# CODY AND THE FRACK-ATTACK PACK

# Cody And The Frack-Attack Pack

TIM STICKLE

Point of Departure Productions LLC.

# Contents

| | | |
|---|---|---|
| 1 | Squeezing The Hoovey | 11 |
| 2 | Pick-A-Fight | 20 |
| 3 | That Sinking Feeling | 30 |
| 4 | Heads of Business | 38 |
| 5 | The Human Zoo | 49 |
| 6 | Don't Let The Goblin Drive | 56 |
| 7 | Backyard Hounds | 65 |
| 8 | A Razzmatazzy Town Meeting | 71 |
| 9 | A Tub of Schramm | 85 |
| 10 | Farmer Redfox's Dark Barn | 93 |
| 11 | Chinny Underestimates | 99 |
| 12 | Urgent Information | 102 |
| 13 | Be Brave In The Cave | 104 |
| 14 | Who Goes There? | 109 |
| 15 | Bumblesquatch The Bear | 111 |
| 16 | King Ridley Kat of Yiddlesmeyer | 114 |
| 17 | Corporate Slimeball | 117 |

| | | |
|---|---|---|
| 18 | Smelly Escape | 121 |
| 19 | A Little Purr-Suasion | 125 |
| 20 | Communication Established | 131 |
| 21 | Mad Cat Dash | 133 |
| 22 | Detonation | 136 |
| 23 | It's Lovely Up Here | 139 |
| 24 | Orchard on Fire | 142 |
| 25 | Fur Ladder To The Sky | 149 |
| 26 | Human Scratching Posts | 152 |
| 27 | Race To The Top | 158 |
| 28 | The Boost | 162 |
| 29 | A Crushing Defeat | 174 |
| 30 | Cody Loves Rumblebarry Pie | 179 |
| 31 | Nocturnal Delight | 184 |

ACKNOWLEDGEMENTS

GLOSSARY

BIBLIOGRAPHY

RESOURCES

ABOUT THE AUTHOR

## CODY AND THE FRACK-ATTACK PACK
### TIM STICKLE

Point of Departure Productions LLC

Point of Departure Productions LLC
6725 Central Ave. Ste M
Toledo, OH 43617
timstickle.com

*This hybrid book is both a work of fiction and nonfiction. The narrative story is fictitious, while the included essays are nonfiction. Other names, characters, places, and events are products of the author's imagination. Any resemblance to actual events or places or persons, living or dead, is entirely coincidental.*

Copyright © 2023 by Tim Stickle

All rights reserved, including the right to reproduce this book or portions thereof in any form whatsoever. For information about permission to reproduce selections from this book, please contact author at: timstickle.com

First Point of Departure Productions edition October 2023

For information about discounts for educational bulk purchases, please contact author at: timstickle.com

Cover and all illustrations by Tim Stickle Copyright © 2023

ISBN 978-1-960677-01-3
ISBN 978-1-960677-00-6 (ebook)

*For my fiercely present Mother*
*Love You Always*

YOU THINK YOU
WALK AWAY...

NOWHERE ELSE TO GO.

**WITHOUT EARTH**
*Illustration by T.L. Stickle*

# Chapter 1

# Squeezing The Hoovey

CHINNY FINSTER POINTED one of his long boney fingers (with the crispy, salty fingernails) at Mayor Hoovenhauer, "Once you're reelected alls you'd have to do is carry out a few simple company directives...in exchange for which we'd be more than happy to keep your campaign coffers flush *now, today.*" The mayor took a few feeble steps away from the warty abomination before him.

"Come on Hoovey, you certainly wouldn't be the first politician to take some special-interest money from the fossil fuel industry." Chinny breathed down on him like a lusty dragon, his breath rank like a sewer.

Finster's words lashed out at him like a thousand little sticky tongues, each grabbing a tiny fistful of his swollen mind so as to pull him closer...and closer. Pressed up against his own desk Hoovenhauer felt cornered, and in his own office no less. Baroo was just below hiding out in the kneehole, his ears pert with attention, at least as pert as any Basset's flippity-floppy ears can ever be.

*Illustration by T.L. Stickle*

So far he'd managed to resist all the greased palms and backroom deals today's pollies were constantly being swayed with, yet Hoovey was starting to crack under the pressure. He wondered if he just might be melting as everything seemed to turn red all around him. Rivulets of sweat cascaded down his meaty brow, the starch in his collar finally admitting defeat.

"*Get with the program,*" Finster leered as he rubbed his thumbs under his index and middle fingers at the beleaguered mayor. The crunchy fingertips made sandpaper kisses as they gently scraped against each other, releasing a barely visible dust...which the mayor inhaled.

Hoovenhauer saw his own reflection begin to change in Finster's large glassy eyes, the left side of his face mottling as if from an inner rot. The other side of the mirror had a different set of intentions altogether...

*On second thought all that easy money would help my re-election for sure: State-of-the-art muckraking TV spots, fancy-schmancy fundraising dinners, posh designer attire, and some great big gulps from a replenished slush fund.*

The *wants* were beginning to course through his veins like black blood as his hands began to tremble.

*Who am I to turn down $300,000 which would serve ME just fine!*

Hoovenhauer's reptilian metamorphosis came on fast, dark green scales violently ripping through his skin like tissue paper. They hardened over his cheeks, plated his brow, and leathered his lips. Splitting right down the middle, his forked tongue darted over his sharp teeth as wanton greed and icy ambition overtook him. His nails were now razor-like talons and he began to drag them across his desk, leaving ragged grooves in the wood.

"*My success would be all but guaranteed...*" the Hoovey-thing hissed.

*Illustration by T.L. Stickle*

He was falling so far so fast through these red skies at night, like a burning star streaking to its death on the horizon.

Then through all the murky blackness, a tiny sound from within his own coffin...

*...scratch-scratch...*

*What?*

*...SCRATCH-SCRATCH...*

Hoovey stopped dropping then, easing his fall until he was bobbing up and down in space as something bright caught his attention.

*...SCRATCH-SCRATCH...*

*BAROO!* It was Baroo under *his desk*...not a coffin after all.

*Grrrrrrrrrrrrrr....*

His big old Basset Hound issued a low growl from below and that brought him back.

That neural pathway - once blocked up in his skull - broke through and began to surge once again as faces emerged out of the gloom...

*There was little Jordan, Alicia, and Melody. David and Michael. Lisa, Chris, Molly, and Vivian. Mary Kay and Marcella. Anne and Esther. Marilyn and Rayna. Debbie and Zach. Martin. Ahmed. So many...*

His scales smoothed over and the dark green color faded.

*There was Siobhan, Brian, Juan, Nina, Trey, Monica, Craig, Amy, and Paul. Brian, Rick, Mrs. Knight, Effie, and Edith McCullough.*

There were people *everywhere* who deserved better.

Breaking the spell, Hoovenhauer snapped a pencil in two, causing Baroo to wince. Hoovey took a deep breath and swallowed. The *cost* of giving in to Finster's unscrupulous demands was too great. Deregulating Timberton's anti-fracking law so as to make some serious bank was signing their environment's death warrant.

Brought back to Chinny's foul presence, newfound clarity washed over Hoovenhauer like fresh spring water.

Did he really want to be just another venal politician?

*No. He did not.*

"And then we'd lose our most precious asset, *our environment*. And along with it, *the Rumblebarry*." Hoovenhauer said, one moment almost drowning in corruption, the next grounded once more. Baroo's tail began to wag.

"That's my Hoovey." Baroo grumbled sweetly.

Chinny's bulbous toad neck puffed out indignantly, "Psphbt! With the kind of loot I'm offering you, you could own your own greenhouse...IN OUTER SPACE!"

Hoovenhauer had finally found his backbone and thankfully (for Timbertonians on both sides of the Borschtissippi River) his moral compass pointed him away from any selfish desires he might've been harboring and redirected him towards the best interests of those he'd sworn to protect. Hoovey's heart swelled up with an earthy paternal love.

*(Thinking of all the compromised aquifers...)*

"When all the *WATER* in Timberton is undrinkable and toxic, the money will be useless." Hoovey countered with sound logic.

Chinny scowled, "You can always..."

*(Thinking of all the wastewater dumping and runoff...)*

"WHEN all the *SOIL* in Timberton is poisoned so that nothing will ever grow in it again, the money will be useless." Hoovey continued.

"Just go buy some artificial plants, they don't need wa..." Chinny said.

(Thinking of all the VOC pollution from the wells...)

"WHEN all the *AIR* in Timberton is unbreathable, the money will be useless." Hoovenhauer spoke with fierce determination.

Chinny grimaced, "You can SELL air too just like on Mars, you fool! Cans of it...all fresh and like...breathable."

Baroo silently snarled at Chinny. Hoovenhauer raised his head, jutting his chin out, "NO, I'm afraid *you* are the fool. Money is ephemeral, a tool that is supposed to *enhance* peoples' livelihoods, not *rob* them of it. Our land here is precious, a true asset. It's not cheap like currency. You can't just go print up some more of it when you run out. You are under the impression I can be bought just like most politicians these days."

Chinny's blank eyes bulged in anticipation, his girthy tongue slathering over his lips. "Well? *Well?!*"

"NO Finster, I can *not*. Your pockets might run deep, but fortunately my sense of integrity runs even deeper. Rumblebarries are indigenous to Timberton in our lush valleys and fertile soils. And they will continue to do so, unthreatened by fracking, which is a completely unnecessary means of energy production. We will stick to *SOLAR* and *WIND POWER* you shortsighted buffoon!"

Baroo nodded his floppy head in stern approval.

Chinny bounced up out of his seat then, suddenly opening one of his corny claws towards Hoovenhauer.

"Know *this* Hoovenhauer. Mayors come and go. And sometimes they go quite fast, if you catch my drift," the claw clenching into an upraised fist. Hoovenhauer only glared at him as he quickly whisked a pen across a pad. Thinking his intimidation was swaying Hoovey, a dry breathy chuckle erupted from Chinny's cavernous pie hole.

Startled by Finster's ghastly laugh, Baroo let out a high-pitched whistle-like whine, catching Finster off guard.

"Whaaaa....?"

When Chinny looked up Hoovenhauer was gone. In his place was an empty desk with a note resting on top. Finster grabbed it and read it aloud, "I *WILL NOT* be seen in public with you. End of story. Mayor Hoovenhauer." Chinny scowled, slowly crumpled up the note and popped it in his gob, swallowing down the declination with a loud gulp. He had a strange urge to dip his fingers in sour cream dip and bite his nails.

Tucking himself even tighter under the desk, Baroo watched Finster as he packed up his stuff into a slimy valise, mumbling his disappointment in a creepy conversation with himself.

"*Don't wanna play the game, huh Hoovey? Well, maybe I just need to play hard ball.*"

Baroo's ears perked up to catch Chinny's sour grumbling with even better reception.

"You *shale* regret betraying me Hoovenhauer," Chinny spewed with a bitter tongue, "Your town will become Chesapuke's new drilling turf *with or without* your help. So at tonight's town meeting, I'll just have to lay it on extra thick." The warty demon cleared his throat, hocked a loogie on Hoovey's ficus, and asked himself in a creepy conspiratorial voice, "How is that going to happen, oh great Chinny-*chin-chin* Finster?"

"*I'll bring out the heavy artillery so as to seduce the gullible townspeople with the old one-two-punch of money and propaganda. These feeble-minded bumpkins will be bought and brainwashed,*" Chinny cackled as he answered himself in a deeper, darker tone, "*and then hung out to dry.*"

His laughter was hollow, cold, and full of spite. Baroo fretted under the desk, that inhuman sound sending shivers up his spine.

"*This time we're playing for keepsss...*" Finster hissed.

*What a hoary cliché, he really is just a bumbling pumpkinhead.* Baroo thought, rolling his eyes in his droopy sockets.

Next a loud drilling sound blared up - another frightful noise to get under Baroo's thick doughy skin. Chinny took out his smart phone and began reading under his breath, sighing in frustration. Baroo grimaced that Chinny would actually use such a grating racket for his phone's text alert.

Yet it fit the scoundrel to a t.

## Chapter 2

# Pick-A-Fight

NESTLED DOWN IN the valley was Timberton's rumblebarry orchard and today was a beautiful day to be working outside. With brilliant sunrays cascading through the canopies of the trees, the entire orchard was ablaze with autumnal color. A soothing warm breeze whispered though the branches, lightly rustling the leaves.

Four solar-powered arbor-drones hummed in their charging bays like kittens purring in their sleep, their panels absorbing the heat of the sun. Once replenished they'd collect a fresh drink from Effie the water tower, to deliver throughout the irrigation network. High above them, like giant pinwheels against a blue sky, the large blades of the wind turbines swept gracefully through the sweet country air, spinning around and around...lulling even a diligent dog into a decidedly drowsy one.

Cody pawed at the air, ascending the heights of a full-fledged fever dream. Grinning from floppy ear to floppy ear, the happy chocolate lab rolled over on his back to hug the Sun.

"CODY!" three dogs barked in unison.

Cody's eyes sprung open to see Mister Sparky, a chubby pug, Skip, a frisky Jack Russell terrier, and Fibbledip, a spazzy

Boston terrier all looking down at him. When Cody just stared at them in bewildered silence, Fibbledip nipped his tail and gave it a good tug.

"Hey!" Cody growled as he was yanked back into reality.

"You kinda looked frozen in time there pal. Had to make sure you were really awake." Fibbledip explained.

"Yeah-Yeah!!" Mister Sparky barked.

Cody rubbed some crusty sleepy winkers from his peepers, coming back to the day.

Skip nodded his head toward the empty baskets. "We've got an hour to fill up those three baskets *or* Aunt Vivian will *not* be making rumblebarry pie – from scratch - this weekend!"

*Silence.*

"That's right," Skip continued, "Before she left to go home and make Timmy's lunch, she let me know the score."

Cody bounced to his paws with renewed vigor. "I want you three dogs to hop up into the tree and shake those branches like you would thrash teddy bears!"

Within moments they had the tree a-shaking and a-shimmering in a berry-dropping dervish like only a pack of pie-hungry chow hounds could. Cody raced back and forth on the ground, catching the plummeting berries in the baskets. The dogs' teamwork was so effective in fact, they finished the job with a good twenty minutes to spare.

From a nearby tree, Mote, a mischievous snow-white rat with beady red eyes, snarled at the dogs down below. Clobber, a quick cat (and Mote's faithful steed) began to whimper and hiss as Mote began to dig his tiny claws into his tender kitty sides a little too roughly.

"Sorry Clobber, but today I've decided those filthy mutts just happen to be the bane of my existence." the trickster rodent said.

Clobber sighed. *Here we go again.*

Mote *was* feeling more sinister than usual. He'd driven Clobber relentlessly through the treetops of the orchards, chuckling as he wrought havoc and chaos. He was a rat though, so causing undue hilarity from time to time was not to be unexpected.

As the rat's claws sunk into his back, Clobber's talon-like nails grasped the branch in a death-grip. Almost invisible amongst the fiery crimson leaves, Mote's beady little red eyes widened as a wicked idea occurred to him.

Loudly clearing his throat: "Well if it isn't Cody-Cobbler, Dog of the Wild Frontier." Mote seethed with sarcasm. "And his little furry flunkies too!" All of the dogs' ears immediately perked up and they were up on their paws in no time.

"Mote!" Cody growled.

The angry rat shook his head from side to side, baring his little vermin teeth in a vicious snarl.

"Hey Cody, maybe you're barking up the wrong tree."

Mote was furious now, his frothy spit hanging off his own whiskers like poisonous dewdrops. He lashed his own tail out as if cracking a whip.

*SNAP! CRACK!*

"Oh great, the little pipsqueak's having another spell." Cody groaned.

"What's that rotten rat up to now?" Mister Sparky wondered aloud.

"Yessssss, yesssssssss," Mote hissed as he eyed the branches thickest with rumblebarries.

Mote picked some, "Now..."

And whipped them down, "...let's make some *JAM*."

Pegging the dogs in a series of kersplats, the no-good rat cackled as he scooped up hearty wads of fresh ammunition.

*SPLAT!*

While Skip and Mister Sparky tried to dodge being pelted, Cody stood perfectly still, impervious to the many rumblebarries smacking down on him. He looked deeply up into the branches, scanning for the exact location of this deadly (and delicious) downpour.

Mote shook his little fist in the air, "That's right Cody, *this is war!* You and your flea-infested posse are all wet. Hahahahahahahaha..."

"Fibbs, Sparky, Skip, form a *Howl Circle* NOW!" Cody barked. All four dogs formed a circle so that they were facing each other. Then their tails made a stiff circling motion, cranking around and around, revving up the canines. One-by-one they began to howl, until they howled in a united voice. "Owwwwwwwwwwwwwwwwwwwwwwwwwwwwwwwwww..." they wailed as the rumblebarries continued to strike them from above.

"That's doing a lot of good," Mote laughed.

Then, again one-by-one, the dogs stopped howling. Only the ker-splats would've been heard then, except when the last dog stopped howling, there was a loud humming from above. All creatures' eyes swept upwards to see four arbor-drones hovering just over the canopy of the trees.

Cody barked once. The four drones whispered high-pitched sighs as they dropped down in front of the dogs.

*Voice-activated? When did they add that feature?* Mote fretted to himself.

"That's right Mote," Cody sneered, "don't bother coming down, we're coming *to you.*" The dogs mounted the arbor-drones; instantly becoming formidable-*ish* air gladiators.

"Break branches for Operation Rat-Smack!" Cody commanded.

The dogs zoomed up into the tree, breaking off wing-sized branches, heavy with fat juicy rumblebarries.

"ABSCOND!" Mote yelled as Clobber booked right out of dodge. People and rodents alike were always in a hurry to get out of that place.

"Sparks and Fibbs: head out to the border and slowly close in from there. Skip and I will chase them, keeping right on their tails." Cody barked as his floppy ears flew behind him.

Clobber sprung from branch to branch with stunning speed and agility. Skip and Cody shadowed them in close pursuit. The feral cat's tail was almost in reach when he vanished down into the dense foliage.

"Duck!" Cody hollered.

Skip turned his head just in time to see one of the wind turbine's giant blades slicing right down towards him.

*SWOOSSSSSSSSSSH!*

Mere inches from getting chopped out of the air, Skip flew right past the blade and – making a sharp U-turn – quickly resumed his chase after Mote. Cody was still slamming on the breaks, tendrils of drool breaking free from his undersnout. Whirling around, Cody felt like he was riding a Frisbee and for a moment thought he might get airsick. *If I blow chunks hopefully it'll be on that rat.*

A powerful surge of restraint then hit him and he took his paw off the accelerator. *One chance just might lead to another.* Cody thought and thus remained hovering above the trees, waiting to see if they would reemerge.

Mote drove Clobber scrambling and diving all around and about the trees, their intense velocity shaking free some giant hairy caterpillars (relatives of Andy Rooney's eyebrows no doubt). No matter how fast they went, they couldn't shake Skip. Using a desperate maneuver, they tried to evade the feisty little dog by ripping through an irrigation feed, hoping to splash him away.

The thrumming of his drone raised in pitch as Skip simply pursued from a higher altitude, easily dodging the kickback.

Cody whipped his head to the right as Mote suddenly popped back up above the orchard's canopy with Skip right on his heels.

Mote was just beginning to feel a false sense of security, seeing the edge of the orchard directly ahead. Much to his ratty chagrin, both Mister Sparky and Fibbledip cut off that escape route and flew towards him. With Cody and Skip right behind him, he was indeed trapped...like a rat.

Completely surrounded, Mote changed tunes. He began smiling at the dogs, shrugging his little furry shoulders in vain.

"I'm a freaking rat. Whadda yah' expect?" he tried to explain.

To say the hovering hounds looked skeptical at the vermin's sudden change of attitude would've been an understatement. Mote tried to weasel himself out of his predicament.

"Look fellas, I was just blowing off some steam, probably too much caffeine. I never meant any ha..." but he was in such deep trouble that even his tics and fleas jumped ship.

"See yah' and I wouldn't wanna be yah!" called Mitzy the Flea as she parachuted off the rat's hide and onto Skip's.

"*PACK-ATTACK!*" Cody ordered.

As if wielding giant flyswatters, all four dogs swung their branches of rumblebarries directly down on Mote and poor old Clobber.

*KER-SPLAT!*

* * * * * * * * * * * * * * * * * * * * * * * * * * * * *

Mote, now wet and purple, twitched his whiskers in defeat as he wrung rumblebarry juice out of Clobber's ever-loving hide, one tiny twist at a time. The battle-fatigued feline meowed and hissed feebly, but the rat showed no signs of stopping.

"Sorry Clobby, but all complaints must be submitted in writing with an SASE attached if you expect an actual response." Mote snarled.

Clobber just sighed and rolled his eyes. From then on the unlikely allies always thought twice - *at least twice* – before attempting to ambush:

## *Cody Cobbler*
## *Dog of the Wild Frontier*

*(Why?)*

Because he was...*THE DOGGEST*

**IT'S TUFF BEING SO RUFF**

*(\*Rated R – pups & runts must be accompanied by a Parrot that Doesn't Talk Back to the Screen or an Adult Giraffe wearing a Really Long Scarf)*

*Illustration by T.L. Stickle*

## Chapter 3

# That Sinking Feeling

BACK AT THE old homestead, in a lush backyard, Cody sat in a wooden tub, covered in suds as his main-mama-human, Aunt Vivian, scrubbed rumblebarry out of his fur.

"Cody, I didn't need you to come gallivanting home with a purple coat on. You ain't Prince, but it sure looks like you got caught in some purple rain!" she growled. Aunt Vivian had a very distinct voice that was gravelly and sweet like honey churning over rocks. Scorn never sounded so lovely.

Truth be told, he was just thinking he ought to come home as a filthy beast more often as his webbed paws practiced their dog-paddle (*splish- splash*). Being a Labrador retriever, he absolutely loved water and this "extra bath" was more than just fine by him, it was *sick joy*.

"Gee whiz Viv; I can't predict random rat-attacks any better than I can predict the weather. We could be tiny people walking through a garden in a jar and I'm sure a storm could find a way of brewing up, even in there!" Cody pleaded.

Vivian considered this for a moment. "Well for one thing, the humidity in there would be unbearable. Next getting a lawnmower through the neck would be neck-st to impossible, require a whole lot of butter and...and..." Then she thought twice: "Ohhh, and that little snowball rat *is* a rascal, no question, but maybe next time you should wear a raincoat while working at the orchard, or maybe...Hush..." she cut herself short as Tweet, Mable, and Din – the three chickadees in her apron - started "PEEPING" loudly.

"There, there," Aunt Vivian cooed as she fed them some birdseed. She kissed some smootchy tweets at them, then looked back up at Cody and furrowed her brow. However, when she saw Cody wince, her face softened again and she sighed.

"I'm sorry for getting so cranky with you Cody; it's just that I'm going through so much right now. I'm really stressed out."

Cody licked her face and wagged his tail, sloshing it through the water. "It's okay Aunt Vivian. I need to try harder sometimes anyway."

Aunt Vivian rubbed her temples, trying to relax.

"Chesapuke, the natural gas company, keeps offering me a lot of cash for a lease to drill on my land. While the money could help out with some things, I ultimately know *the cost is too high.*" she sighed. She then gently took Cody's ears in her hands and flapped them up and down, sending a few spry bubbles floating off into the breeze.

"As much as I would like to tell you all their persuasion just goes in one ear and out the other, that's not altogether true. Some of it gets stuck in my head, where it festers like a dark temptation."

Cody frowned, "The money won't last and neither will Nature since we both know how much irreparable damage fracking can do to the environment. Just like me, don't you want your energy clean too?"

"I know, but all that fast cash keeps me second-guessing myself in a really annoying way. That's just the sad truth for now." She then hugged him close to her. "Let's both hope I do the right thing."

*Illustration by T.L. Stickle*

Cody leaped out of the tub and began to do a spazzy shake-it-off dance, flinging water everywhere. After using a towel as a shield, Vivian quickly embraced him in it where he squirmed happily. As he dried off, he saw Timmy, his little-boy-human, across the yard playing by the brook.

The six-year-old picked up his toy sailboat and gently set it on the water. It bobbed up and down and if it strayed too far from shore, it would surely be grabbed by the current and taken far down stream, which eventually fed into the Muir River.

This grassy spot by the ravine was Timmy and Cody's favorite. With its lush flora, trickling stream, and irresistible tranquility it was easy to see why. Some days – like today - the cat-o'-nine-tails would gently sway and bob in the breeze, almost lulling them into an afternoon nap.

Cody felt at peace watching him play. He understood how nourishing this experience was for the both of them, a deep sense of unity between them and Nature. Taking a long sigh, Cody remembered and appreciated just how clean the air was here. Feeling thirsty, he trotted down to the water's edge and helped himself to a hearty drink, also loving just how pure the water still was as well.

Cody's smile froze and then melted into a frown as Aunt Vivian's doubt haunted his mind.

*As much as I would like to tell you all their persuasion just goes in one ear and out the other, that's not altogether true. All that cash is a real temptation all the same. Let's both hope I do the right thing.*

Timmy bellowed out a harsh cry. Cody looked up to see the poor little boy yanking his hand from the stream, his skin burning as if dipped in acid. The river was now a steaming pool of stagnant brown and pink filth. Dead fish bobbed on the surface just before they were sucked down into the lost river.

"Make it stop! Make it stop! It burns! *IT BURNS!*" Timmy screamed, flailing his hand through the air. The toxic river sludge was quickly burning through Timmy's arm like sizzling gravy, the bones already exposed. Cody frantically looked around, but there was no relief to be found.

*I hope his parents can afford to buy him a hook.*

A few muddy bubbles splattered from the top of the sludge. Then two slimy antennae rose out of the viscous ooze followed by the spotted head of a giant slug dripping with red eyes...

*...SCHLERG!*

As if to herald his arrival, the reeds whispered in the wind:

*Oh Great Schlerg*
*In all your snot drenched divinity*
*You are ample proof*
*America's undrained swamps*
*Are capable of producing*
*Some truly formidable specimens*

*Schlarby Gorsucks, Prooit, Squealer*
*Have proudly followed your slimy scorched trail of*
*Wanton environmental degradation*
*Bulbous. Putrescent. Magnificent.*
*You are more than a mere invertebrate*
*You defile the land for profit making all*
*The fossil fuel flunkies cheer*

THE END IS NEAR! THE END IS NEAR!

*Illustration by T.L. Stickle*

Then the river *was* Schlerg, its path instantly blackening the grass. A toxic burning stench wafted from the pustulent serpent, its wet hide glistening in the sour sun. Neither boy nor dog could manage to catch a breath of fresh air. They both tried to back up, but sank instead, the ground dissolving into quicksand. From ankle-deep to knee-deep, the more they struggled, the deeper they sunk into the suffocating schlerping schlarb.

The giant slime-ridden worm heaved its putrid bulk to and fro, writhing toward the quagmire hoping to devour the brat and mutt. Gelatinous Schlerg was considering becoming a vegan...*but not today.*

Today *meat* was required.

*Puh-dum...*

*Illustration by T.L. Stickle*

Knowing the end was near; Timmy hugged Cody awkwardly with his remaining arm and smootched his snout. Schlerg had reached the edge of the quagmire and was mere inches from them, its wriggling antennae almost brushing Cody's back. If the sandy death pudding didn't eat them alive, the rancid worm would surely swallow them whole.

*Puh-dum... Puh-dum...*

Cody laid his furry paws on the boy's trembling shoulders, trying to comfort him, despite his own doggie tears. Timmy only looked him dead in the eyes and said, "Puh-doodoo, Bobbaloo!"

"*What?*" Cody barked, totally confused.

Timmy was sputtering gibberish along with the babbling brook. As Baroo gave his tail a good tug, Cody was yanked back into reality (hopefully not a fleeting one this time) and wagged his tail at seeing his good friend again. Cody jumped on Baroo, nipping at his drooping ears.

"Hey, don't cuddle the messenger!" Baroo squawked.

"What message is that?" Cody asked.

"Unfortunately a bad one. Chinny Finster - that putrid parasite from the natural gas company - is planning to brainwash all of Timberton at tonight's town meeting. And he's bringing some serious suds!"

"Hmmm..." Cody pondered this predicament. His tail slowly wagged from side to side as he devised a course of action.

"What should we do?" Baroo asked.

"Tell all the other dogs we're having an emergency meeting at four o'clock right here in my back yard." Cody instructed Baroo. "Have every dog you tell go run and tell another. You'll cover more ground that way."

"Awesome! So why don't you come with me?"

"I need to stay here and think up some plans. From the sound of it, they better be rock-solid if we're gonna throw a wrench into Chinny's Big Bamboozle tonight."

"Gotcha," Baroo said. "I'll see you back here in a few hours with the crew. Hey Cody, do you mind if I grab a sip from your water dish before I scram?"

"As long as you don't backwash." Cody laughed.

Baroo took a couple slurps, tripped on one of his own long drooping ears, then got back up and scrambled out into the neighborhood to spread the word.

# Chapter 4

# Heads of Business

HIS PARANOIA MOUNTING, Chinny began to see faces everywhere. Speaking of which, was that Honest Abe down there? While most definitely not one of his heroes, he spotted a cruddy old penny stuck in a sidewalk crack and bent over to retrieve it. Feeling a sudden chill, he turned his head to see a dilapidated warehouse...which appeared to be watching him with keen interest.

*Illustration by T.L. Stickle*

Right side up wasn't any better. Just the sight of it took the pep out of Chinny's step, and his pace slackened the closer he got...especially after he thought he saw a broken window winking at him. His bugged out eyes took in the faded green street sign reading "Dedtree Avenue."

*Illustration by T.L. Stickle*

Giving the ominous building a wide berth, Finster wound his way toward the back where he reached the loading docks which were adorned with such lively graffiti as: "HAIR OF THE DOG LIFTS THE MORNING FOG!" along with "THAT TREE'S BARK IS WORSE THAN IT'S BITE" spray-painted in lurid greens and dismal browns.

His feet were practically cemented to the ground. Regardless of this being a prearranged meeting, entering this hellish building struck him as incredibly foolhardy. Yet - finally casting his reluctance aside - he crept through a back door, noticing it had been left slightly ajar. He spotted a bright yellow arrow made out of tape on the wall to his left. It pointed him forward and down to another corridor which went in both directions. There another yellow arrow pointed him to the right. A couple of rats rushed by as if scampering away from something.

Next he came to a staircase with a sharp-pointed yellow arrow directing him upwards. Chinny scowled as the rickety iron stairs trembled under his corpulent bulk, chips of rust shaking loose to fall like reddish-brown snowflakes. His barking hamstrings made him wonder if his pencil-thin legs just might snap. He grumbled between his panting breaths.

A large crumbling brick wall was at the top, a final yellow arrow pointing him once again to the right. Chinny walked into what had to be the warehouse's most spacious room, careful not to trip on the warped wooden floor. High above dark thorny vines hung from broken windows in the ceiling.

Peering into the darkness trying to get a better grasp of the place, he took a few steps forward and stopped. Rummaging in his vest pocket, he took out four small silver discs –holographic projectors. He set them in a large semi-circle and then stepped back. A few dusty pigeons beat their wings and cooed restlessly as they flew out of the room.

Fidgeting with his tie, Finster spat into his palm and then ran it through his frizzy purple hair as he struggled to make himself presentable. By a stroke of bad luck, he caught a glimpse of his gruesome self in a shard of broken glass. His shoulders lurched backward as he cringed, and then eased into a more casual shrug.

"It's what's inside that counts," he chuckled under his breath, his bulbous eyes rolling in their sockets. One of his crispy fingers drew something curvy in the air – slashing two streaks through it - then touched the "ENGAGE" button on his phone.

All four discs generated an electric humming noise as they quickly powered up. Then each disk's cover irised open, revealing lenses pulsing with bright cold blue light. Four fugly faces rose up like ghastly genies, the tops of their heads almost brushing the ceiling.

Chinny stood uneasily before the interactive holograms, his pointy knees starting to buckle. Each face towered high above him. He found himself feeling guilty under their harsh gazes. The giant disembodied heads hovered around him like demented parade balloons.

"Well, how did the meeting with the mayor of Tinytown go?" Dom Corbutt – a pasty n' puffy ape - asked. "Surely he was persuaded by our generous offer?"

"Unfortunately, he's not the pushover snollygoster we originally pegged him for." Chinny explained, shrugging.

Another head made up of two crusty haggard faces sewn together with a crude Frankensteinian suture glared at him with cold contempt.

"A polly..." one half of the (Sick) Joke Brother's face started, only to have the second half chime in, "...who's not a snolly?!?" with stark disbelief.

"Sssssstrange..." the gruesome twosome hissed.

Plick Insaney, a moldy bespectacled hog, cut in, "They sort of have a...*built-in* rapacious quality you can count on. Trust me; nobody knows that better than *Me*." as he shuffled a deck of C-notes under his nose, fervently sniffing while licking his puckered piehole.

"Maybe those rare pollies with actual integrity aren't as extinct as we thought." Chinny countered.

"Don't you get it Finster?" Gleter Drabreck - a wax figure with a pulse - explained. "The more pervasive fracking is, the more contaminated the water becomes. Then the local bumpkins have no choice *but to pay* to have it shipped in to them from an outside supplier. WATER SCARITY IS A BUSINESS TOO. The future *is* water privatization."

"Yes, yes, a water dealer." Chinny agreed.

"Drought-Schmought!" Corbutt exclaimed. "With Senate Bill 4, our fracking operations' water use superseded the public's. Our Cali wells were sucking up to as much as six million gallons

of water *EACH*, while the public was under strict rationing." He cackled, "We were untouchable. And with a little more cooperation one day *we will own the rain*. Hell, if I can gear my state's conservation funding so that it actually has to rely on fracking...well, then the sky's the limit."

"He seems to be aware of all the potential environmental hazards that come with fracking. He seems to think that the land, air, water and earth are more valuable than money." Chinny said.

"Looks like the mayor's a smart man." Insaney said, beginning to snort laughter. The others joined him in a conspiratorial chuckle.

"But wealth has a strange way of trumping logic..." one of the Joke Brothers seethed through the left side of their mouth.

"...every time." the other Joke Brother squawked from the right, trying to seize control of their shared speaker-box.

"And in those rare cases where money actually doesn't talk..." one of the heads spoke up, "...forceful will can – *and does* - speak volumes, if you catch my drift." It then opened its pie hole even wider and dropped a poor bewildered (and spiced) apricot toad into it, gobbling it down whole.

Chinny licked his foul chops, his warty tongue savoring even the mention of such good old school criminality. For today's modern-day criminality was completely sanctioned by the federal government and all of its agencies (which had been bought and paid for by Big Oil, Wall Street, Big Tech and the rest of the countries' most powerful corporations) and thus, it had all the fun taken out of it.

White-collar crime was so commonplace these days it left Finster, well...*cold*. He was left yearning for the blunt steaming flavor of conspicuous crime: armed robberies, wanton destruction of another's property, and savage brutality. Alas, complicity was so pervasive today, there really wasn't much effort required anymore. Chinny needed to get back to his roots like the black-hearted scoundrel he was, and this might be just the opportunity to indulge in some good old-fashioned maiming.

"Of course, I'm always willing and able my liege." Chinny grunted eagerly, cracking his knuckles. "I'll gladly rip them to shreds, if you so desire. Then cover my tracks, leaving without a trace..." He shivered as the coldness finally hit him. His beady eyes rolled downwards as he noticed his rank breath had become visible smoke. He still had the dragon, only now he could see it flying about himself on blue wings.

*Illustration by T.L. Stickle*

In this frigid zone, where humans were only valued according to their economic worth and nothing else, the temperature of the room (already cold) continued to plummet. Crackling blisters of ice grew and stretched across the ceiling and walls. As a loud frost scarred the glass of the unbroken windows, large icicles quickly formed over them like arctic prison bars.

Clanking pipes rumbled through the walls sinking their way down to subterranean depths – where they would go quiet – only to have clinking chains, heavy and reluctant with rust, click and scrape as they were slowly pulled up through the roof into the cold grey sky. A shard of glass fell from one of the ceiling's windows, hitting the floor with a shattering echo.

"I can see your future now Mr. Finster." Drabreck cooed, donning a pair of large puffy green earmuffs.

Chinny's rotten mind wandered a little as his eyes left the phantasmagorical faces to trace their beams back down to the hologram generators. He could feel the electrical pulsating of each disk, like cold hearts beating in the darkness. What if he grabbed them and threw them through one of those broken windows?

*Who would I be then?* A fleeting thought zipped through his thick head.

"...yachts, a home in the Hamptons, a swanky penthouse in the city, any luxury car you could ever imagine...just no hybrids please, they're bad for our business..." the Joke Brothers spewed on as it/they slathered waxy lip balm on their shared sourpuss.

"All the trimmings befitting a king." Corbutt croaked while chomping down on a phantom banana.

"Or squalor and abject poverty awaits *YOU* if you dare fail us." Insaney warned with malicious glee. Old Plick then sneezed loudly – his head bobbing in the blue electrical light. He then blew his nose on a green hanky, adding, "Serving defense contractors is money well spent - NOT public education. Wars can be easily manufactured with such widespread fear and ignorance via Weapons of Mass Deception. If by chance you need to resort to even more drastic measures...say you need heavier ammunition of all sorts. Well, fret not. I've got connections."

"I wouldn't doubt it." Chinny agreed.

"We have the FDA, the EPA, and the White House in our pockets, so make no mistake; we are running the show now," he squealed and snorted.

"This entire country's political system is now at our beck and call." Dom Corbutt said. "And we intend to wield that power to further our interests." He then put on a warm wool hat with two holes at the top so his greasy horns could slide right through.

"No regulations should *ever* stand in the way of our profits." the Joke Brothers hissed. "And I'm sure you can tell, we've done an excellent job of fast-tracking and deregulating any ridiculous policies implemented to benefit such lost causes as the general public and the environment."

"Crimes against water notwithstanding, DP and Hexxon still reap billions of dollars of profit. So regardless of massive oil spills and other such contaminations of our oceans, they remain unscathed. And so shall we." Gleter Drabreck gloated.

"See, we're not just corporations anymore, we're real people." Corbutt snorted. "Especially now that we also have the Supreme Court doing our bidding as well."

"So Finster, are we on the same page?" Drabreck demanded.

"Yes, yes we are!" Chinny slurped.

"Either you get us all of that land for fracking – and clearly, we don't care *how* you go about doing it – OR you'll be a common man once again. And you know what *that* means don't you?" Corbutt said.

A series of sharp crackles could be heard as Chinny's sweat froze right to his brow as he nodded.

"That's right: You'll be paying a *much higher* tax rate than the wealthy, you'll never have any job security again, and you'll never see another pay raise or pension again in your lifetime. Even working full time, you will still be just below poverty level, not living but merely existing as just another wage slave. How does that sound?" the Joke Brothers taunted.

Chinny was frozen still.

"Don't be so nervous," Insaney spoke, "this isn't enhanced interrogation...*yet*."

Swallowing as if trying to find his voice, Chinny uttered, "It sounds like a rotten deal, a total rip-off."

The Heads of Business all bellowed deafening laughter, so loud it set off zigzagging streaks of cracks throughout the icy walls and ceiling.

"I concur wholeheartedly Mr. Finster...it certainly is." Insaney grunted a few last snorts.

"Clearly we would never want to see you down and out," Corbutt seethed and smirked.

"You always were thirsty for new chances to prove your worthiness," Drabreck chimed in, licking his chapped lips.

"We're presenting you with one hell of an opportunity here Finny. *Don't muck it up.*" Insaney warned.

"Ssssssso get it done." the Joke Brothers hissed in unison.

The ultimatum handed down; each head zapped itself out as the hologram generators powered down.

...*zzzzzppppphhhttttt!*

As more shards of glass and slivers of ice crashed down from the ceiling, Finster sprung open his umbrella and retrieved the silver discs.

Before departing he glanced once again at one of the broken windows.

## Chapter 5

# The Human Zoo

DAGMAR – A GREAT Dane fell behind as she froze in her tracks. Slowly, she turned her head to the left as she saw a large creepy man in a striped apron - Bilge Conners - across the boardwalk leering at her. In his grimy hands he held a fistful of balloons and a bunch of coloring books.

"Cwans! Cwans! I'm gonna need cwans mama!" cried Vinter, a little boy who ran up to him with his mother close behind. Bilge's face instantly transformed from super-creep to normal, jolly zoo employee (but without a name badge). Dagmar watched with guarded fascination.

"Mommy you buy me a cahwahing book!" the boy said.

"Sir, how much are the coloring books?" the mother asked.

"The coloring books AND balloons are FREE!" Bilge replied, as he handed one of each over to the eager child.

"What a nice man! That's very sweet of you. Now Vinter, what do we say?" the mother asked her child.

Vinter looked up at Bilge and smiled, "Thanks big guy."

Bilge smiled back, but it was a shark's smile. "You're very welcome small fry, but thank Chesapuke NRG as *they* are the providers of today's treats."

Once the mother and son had moved on, Bilge's real face returned and he gave a creepy nod towards the dogs.

"I don't like him one bit." Cooper, a frisky Siberian husky, said.

"Safe to say none of us do." Maisey, an alert German shepherd, added.

"Sat's a face only sie mutter kould lofe." Dagmar declared.

"Yeah, maybe a blind mother." Smokey, a rascal of a Dachshund, cooed.

They all giggled and walked on to another exhibit.

They stopped in front of a Polly Paddock. Looking into the stone enclosure, they saw old gas station pumps and dirty tires everywhere. They noticed some movement as their attention shifted to a giant tractor tire where two spindly legs emerged, followed by the crazed head of a miserable old man. He threw them a scornful look, licked at something, and then proceeded to pick lint out of his bellybutton. The dogs kind of shrugged and then looked at the sign posted inside of his enclosure:

*Illustration by T.L. Stickle*

*Illustration by T.L. Stickle*

*Meet Georgie the Polly!*
*Species: Typical Politician (Venal Vermin)*

- *Allowed Homelessness to run rampant while preferring: Golf Courses, Boarded Up Buildings, and New Cemeteries. Was allowed/encouraged to make regular egregious decisions – such as pouring more money into prisons while shortchanging schools - in the name of profit instead of looking out for society's best interests. Allowed Corporations to buy up his political will in favor of his own personal interests. Vehemently denied climate change at the command of his corporate masters (fossil fuel industry). Was emboldened into corruption and mendacity through the dysfunctional political system humans sadly still try to maintain and operate in today. Due to the petrification of his heart and the lazy trappings of his mind, Georgie is now on display here at The Human Zoo.*

The dogs frowned and some even whimpered, all of them truly crestfallen. A tear ran down Maisey's cheek, "We need space for the living, *not* for frivolous games or the dead." She looked over at the miserable polly slumped in its tire and raised her voice, "Why didn't you try to open any of those buildings so to create some humane spaces for the homeless to stay?"

"Why is punishment more of a priority than education?" Smokey wanted to know.

"Dit you efen kare about sie people voo elekted you?" Dagmar asked.

"**When you were accepting all those bribes?**" Maisey said, raising her voice.

"How could you even begin to try to deny global warming?" Cooper barked.

Georgie only held up a yellow snow cone and yelled, "*See,* this is *proof* that climate change is just a big hoax!"

Dagmar grimaced, "ahem...schnar-rowl oont groaw-wal."

The ripe zoo air wafted over the dogs' snouts like *mind-stink.*

"Double-Dud," Cooper growled, instantly realizing the futility of arguing with a paid liar.

Smokey regarded the miserable human in the cage then looked over to a mother pushing her young child up to have a peek at the bad example inside. "Why are some humans locked up and some aren't? I thought this place was a zoo. It's more like a jail."

"*Sese* humans here are scho deadly in seir avarice ant deschire for pover, sat say represchent exchtreme schreats to *all* schpecies on Urs, inkludink seir own." Dagmar explained in a salty wry tone. "It's edukational *here,* scho it's sie zoo."

Smokey gazed at her with intense curiosity.

"Vur learnink vrom sie humans' krimes/mischtakes. *But if pandasch, zebrasch, lionsch, ant oser animalsch ver in sese kages, sen* it vould be sie jail, schince seir only krime vould be exischting in see firscht place."

Smokey slightly nodded and frowned.

"Are vee schimpatico Schmokey?" she asked.

"Yes Daggie, we are and now I understand completely: Regardless of its purpose, a cage is still a cage meant to imprison another living creature and deny it their freedom."

"Ant cages only efer komes from *ant belongs to* humans. It's zer vay."

Smokey then raised his two front paws, tapping one on his head and the other on his chest. "The worst cages are always in here."

Dagmar sighed wistfully, "Yesch, in your mynt ant in your heart. Sose are sie abscholute vorst."

Smokey noticed a little pink tag hanging off Georgie's exhibit sign. He read it, and then asked, "Hey guys, what does 'PTS scheduled for 6/7/24' mean?"

In a hushed tone, Dagmar answered, "It meansch, 'Puten to Schleep.'"

"Ohhh, like he's got insomnia?" Smokey said.

Sighing, Dagmar continued, "No you schilly veiner dawg, it meansch sey vill killen him in a humane manner scho asch to maken room for more."

"Bummer." Maisey said, "Imagine what they could've been."

"And what they settled on instead." Cooper solemnly replied. *Big fun at the zoo.*

Baroo suddenly zipped around a corner, crashing into the gang, creating one giant furball in the process.

*Harrumph!*

"Gu...guys...did you...did you see Bilge," Baroo was panting for breath.

"See what? The miserable humans? Yes, in fact I'd say we've gotten our fill for the day." Smokey snapped.

"NO!" Baroo barked. "*The man!* The creepy dude with the balloons!"

"OHHH HIM!" they answered in unison.

"Yesch, ant he's one schcary kreep!" Dagmar exclaimed, kicking out her back right leg.

"He's one of Chinny's henchmen!" Baroo barked up.

"Well, I don't know Baroo," Cooper said, "he was giving away free balloons and coloring books to kids."

"Take a closer look." Baroo said as he passed one of the coloring books to Cooper. All the dogs looked down at a *PRO-FRACKING coloring book*. On the cover was a hydraulic fracking drill with the end of a rainbow centered directly on its bit as it bore into the ground.

"*NOOOOoooooooooo!*" they all howled.

"That's right, the corporate flunkies are using propaganda to persuade the kids and their parents to buy into their pro-fracking agenda." Baroo said.

"Crafty devils!" Smokie exclaimed.

"And that's not all, not by far," Baroo continued. "Tonight Chinny and his crew are having a town meeting in order to further persuade folks into leasing their land for fast cash. And of course he'll forget to bring up any of the environmental consequences I'm sure."

"Which means?" Cooper asked.

"Which means *WE* are having our own town meeting *first* at four o'clock in Cody's back yard. So we can counterattack Chinny's propaganda with some real information." Baroo answered right back.

"How dit you efer get scho schmart?" Dagmar asked.

"I've eaten a lot of homework in my life." Baroo said.

"I bet your owner has taken a lot of words right out of your mouth," Maisey giggled, "especially when you were trying to chew up his dictionary!"

All the dogs including Baroo laughed at this oldie-but-goodie.

Baroo was the first to stop however. His ears perked up as he spotted Bilge lumbering towards them.

"We need to get out of here NOW!" Baroo shouted.

"Why?" Maisey asked.

"Because here comes Bilge! And he's also a *dogcatcher!* Don't forget: Four o'clock at Cody's. Tell everyone you can!"

The dogs scampered away in five different directions, making it impossible for nasty old Bilge to follow them anymore. He grimaced and spat a green loogie out of his foul gob. Then he began to blow up another yellow balloon with his helium tank. However, instead of tying it with a string, he stretched its rubbery mouth open and inhaled deeply so his voice became an obnoxiously animated high-pitched sputtering.

"Rotten furballs, always poking their wet noses in other peoples' business. When I cast my net, they'll make an epic catch." he chuckled.

Chapter 6

# Don't Let The Goblin Drive

THERE THEY WERE: his favorite treats! He knew they were his favorites too because he saw the shiny blue bag they always came in sitting on Max's desk...

*Waaaaaay up there on top of Max's desk.*

From under the folds of his doggie bed, the Chihuahua, Spatchcock, looked up over to the bag – and licked his chops – and then at the clock on the wall:

*One o'clock, still a couple of hours before his little boy would be back from school. Plenty of time to sneak-a-snack.*

Spatch's cute little tummy rumbled as temptation beckoned him to a challenge. His eyes scanned the room, hunting for an opportunity to make this work: basketball, pile of dirty clothes, toys, shoes, chair, desk, trashcan, backpack...

*The chair!*

Yes, the chair would provide just enough height to allow him to reach the top of the desk. He would have to somehow climb up to its seat first and even higher up to one of its arms – using it as a sort of diving board – and then leap over to the treats. Unfortunately earlier this morning – when Max yanked his jacket off the back of it – it had rolled out and being in such a hurry, he had neglected to tuck it back in under the desk.

Having to not only reach the chair's seat, but then actually leap from it all the way over to the desk made him queasy. See, Spatchcock just didn't like heights, they made him woozy. Max was careful not to pick him up too high off the ground, so as not to trigger his vertigo. Despite this, the tiny dog once more let his eyes travel from the carpet on up to the chair and up and over to the desk and the treats.

*As long as I remember not to look down, I really don't have anything to worry about.*

His tummy rumbled again and he shrugged his shoulders.

*Okay, I'm doing this.*

Very quietly he lifted the edge of the blanket so he could check for monsters under Max's bed.

"Hello?" he barked into the darkness

No reply, but he did find a note:

*We're in the basement for a pep rally, so you're safe...for now. Love, The Monsters.*

Spatchcock sighed relief.

The coast appeared to be clear, so Spatchcock darted into the cave and used all his might to shove out an old shoe box – filled with Max's comic book collection – next to the chair. He then looked from the top of the box to the seat of the chair.

*That's just not gonna cut it.*

The little Chihuahua rescanned the room until his eyes landed on the bulky plastic thing with all the buttons on it which Max was always pointing at that weird (and very noisy) screen. It had a wire attaching it to an even bulkier (and much heavier) box-like thing, which he quickly unplugged. Dragging the whatchamacallits by its cord, he then pushed it on top of the shoe box and once again checked his progress.

*Almost but not quite.*

(scanning in progress...please wait...)

*There!*

In a pile of toys, he spotted a little barrel of slimy gunk that Max loved to mold into random things. Delighted, Spatch wagged his furry banana tail a couple of times as he began to dig out the last step he needed to reach the seat.

His bat wing ears twitched as he thought he heard something shift in the pile. After a moment of stillness, he rolled the barrel over to his makeshift stairs and used his hind legs to push it up onto the shoe box. He then heaved himself on top of it as well.

*"Click! Shhhhhhhhhhhhhhhhhhhhhhh...."*

Spatch yelped as the TV turned itself on to a dead channel of snowy static and loud white noise. He pressed his little body low to the shoe box.

*Illustration by T.L. Stickle*

A big dark hand swinging in and out of the milky electro fuzz *tap-tap-tapping* against the inside of the screen. The TV slightly shifted on its stand. Frozen and terrified, Spatch's eyes were glued to the tube. Slowly, a toothy commercial spokesman emerged with a red straw and sucked up all the static.

"Scrumptious!" he belched.

Leering, he pointed at Spatch.

*What could you possibly be doing, you naughty dog!*

Spatchcock pressed his head down even harder against the cardboard box.

*Do you want to break little Max's heart when you wind up killing yourself for a lousy treat?*

Spatch certainly didn't, but at the same time, he wasn't exactly sure of what station he was watching. He closed his eyes and proceeded to lift the barrel on top of the plastic whatchamacallits. Gently, he placed a paw and then another on the plastic thingy which was becoming increasingly wobbly. He began to slide off a bit, so he grabbed a couple of the buttons to keep his place.

The seat was getting closer, so he very carefully climbed atop the barrel of gunk which began to tremble under his weight.

*Don't do it! You will die! Don't do it! You will die! Don't do it!*

A wind-up robot repeated its dire warning as it emerged from the pile of toys, its gears crunching with every step. Spatch took a breath and jumped. Landing in Max's seat, the chair swiveled around several times and he thought he'd just taken a spin on the Tiki Twirl. The ride was over, but Spatchcock was still spinning so he closed his eyes.

*Don't look down.*

*Don't look down.*

*Don't look down.*

He took a long breath, stepped in place a few times, and opened his eyes. Feeling he'd regained his sense of balance, he climbed onto the chair's right arm. Now barely two feet away, he could see the bag of treats just waiting for him.

*...yyyaaaaaaggggaaaaahhhhhhnnnaaaaafaaaaaahhhhh...*

A soft murmuring somewhere in the distance caught his attention.

...*yaaaaahhhhhggggaaaaaannnahhhhhhhffffaaaaaaaa*.....

Louder this time. Spatchcock turned his head and waaaaaaaaay across the gaping canyon between the desk and the top of Max's bed, he saw funny little Franklin – Max's favorite teddy bear – sitting on the edge of the bed.

...*yoooooorrrrrggggguuunnnnaaafaaaaaaaahhhhl*....

*Illustration by T.L. Stickle*

Franklin wasn't very funny today.

*He's downright creepy in fact.* Spatchcock thought before looking back at the bag of treats. He knelt down on his haunches, readying himself to pounce on over to his just rewards.

*HEY!*

Spatchcock sighed and looked over at Franklin.

*YOU'RE GOING TO FALL!*

Franklin jumped off the edge of the bed.

"Nooooo!" cried Spatchcock.

The fuzzy bear hit the carpet with a soft landing and then looked up at Spatchcock.

*Just remember to NEVER look down.*

Just like the twist of a key, Spatchcock's vertigo was unlocked. He saw Franklin *waaaaaaaaaaaaaay* down there on the floor, and the floor came rushing back up at him like the charge of a bull. The tiny dog quickly lifted his head and closed his eyes, but it was too late. He started lumbering from side to side, his paws desperately trying to keep their purchase on the chair arm, finally dropping straight down into Max's trash can.

*PLOP!*

Luckily a slew of Max's candy wrappers and crumpled-up homework papers cushioned his fall. Spatchcock scowled as he heard Franklin laughing at him, and he jumped up out of the can.

"HEY!"

"Hey Spatch, what's shaking?!"

*My ever-loving hide!* Spatch thought for a second, before he realized it was his friend Clover, a feisty beagle.

"I thought you were my teddy bear!" Spatchcock exclaimed.

"That's very affectionate of you." Clover barked.

"Uhhh..."

"What are you doing inside on such a beautiful day?" she asked.

Spatch, still dazed, looked around the room, "Failing miserably to score some treats."

"Why are you inside that trash can?"

"It's a long story. Sorry Clover. I kind of feel down today."

"Why? What's wrong?"

"I'm such a loser Clover, my fears keep dragging me down...literally at times..."

"Spatchcock, you are *not* a loser, not by far."

"The loudest voice in my head keeps telling me I am, and I guess the more I hear it, the more I believe it." Spatch frowned.

"Okay Spatch, I need you to listen up real good." Clover announced, tugging on one of his ears. "Because I'm going to hip you to one of life's unpleasant truths."

"You mean there's even more?" Spatch grumbled.

"Shhh...listen." Clover soothed her friend. "Everybody and I mean *everybody* has a nasty little goblin living inside his or her own head. This sucker wallows in negativity and if left unchecked, will gladly run amok - taking you hostage on its latest road trip to the magical land of Self-Defeating Chaos."

"Sounds less than magical if you ask me." Spatch chimed in.

"You better believe it. See, this goblin is pretty fierce and bullheaded and wants to be in the driver's seat *all the time*. Think of him as sort of an evil auto-pilot. He's one hell of a reckless driver. So much so, he should *never* drive...yet, sadly most of us allow him to do just that."

"Guilty as charged."

"Ditto. Anyway, you need to rip your own steering wheel out of his rotten clutches *any* and *every time* he tries to start driving YOU."

"Why?"

"First of all, because he *always* wants to drive you someplace you *just* don't wanna go. And when and if you get there, he's going to make sure you crash...*every time.*"

"Well, how do I do that?!" Spatch squealed. "Am I supposed to revoke his license or something?"

Clover tilted her head thoughtfully to one side for a moment. "In a matter of speaking, *yes*. This negativity goblin will increase in volume, becoming louder and louder the more attention you pay him."

"Earplugs?"

"Better yet, sucker punch him in the gut until he backs down, becoming nothing but some background noise."

"His proper place?"

"Exactly."

"What if he's stronger than me? And I still become negative?" Spatch asked cautiously.

"You'll develop more strength over time by rerouting all that energy down a new neural pathway."

"How do I create a new neural pathway?"

"Do you have a spike and hammer?" the sassy beagle bugged her eyes out and let her tongue loll down one side of her snout.

Spatch only looked at her completely aghast.

"*Just kidding!* With enough patience you'll quickly recognize your own routine and then learn how to block yourself." Clover smiled.

"Block myself?"

"Yes, block yourself from going the wrong way. YOU are going to create a new pathway within yourself. Keep at it and you'll travel in style too."

"But what if I don't?"

"If you choose not to, you'll sadly wind up becoming your own worst enemy, imprisoned in your own mind. Remember Spatchcock, *the idea* is to stop giving him power and to give it *to yourself* instead."

"I don't want to spend my entire life running around chasing my own tail. Besides, I'm tired of having a crick in my neck from looking over my shoulder all the time." Spatch lamented, perfectly dour.

"Look at it this way; life's not some perfect puzzle you have to fit in to. You have to find yourself, be yourself, and then *love yourself unconditionally*. Like only a dog can do."

"I think I could do that."

"*Know you can* my friend. Trust me, you're going to learn to let go, and life will be so much better from then on." Clover encouraged him. "Just always remember, Spatch..."

"Remember what?"

"*Do not* let the goblin drive. Hell, don't even let him ride shotgun!"

Spatch smiled as his ears perked up. "Why *are* you here again?"

"Because I need your help."

"What can I do? I scare easily." Spatchcock started to fret a little.

Clover lightly knocked Spatch's chin up, "I wouldn't be asking you, if I didn't believe in you. And my friend, *YOU can do a lot*. So come on, Spatch, I met up with Baroo earlier and we have to help round up the rest of Timberton's dogs for an emergency meeting."

"What for?"

"There's a *new* goblin in town."

# Chapter 7

# Backyard Hounds

CODY WAS READY for the emergency meeting. The backyard fence's gate was open, and he sat upright on his haunches waiting for his friends and neighbors to arrive. This chocolate Labrador retriever was a natural-born leader and today he was determined to show his chops (instead of just lick them).

First to arrive was a big Rhodesian ridgeback named Sally. Next came Smokey the Dachshund accompanied by Marsha, a perfectly smootchy Pit Bull, and Dagmar the Great Dane. A new dog with a stunning spotted coat hopped in next with a couple of frisky friends. Cody came up and introduced himself.

"I'm Cody and I'm putting on today's meeting. Haven't seen you guys before have I?" Cody asked the strange new dogs, after a few investigative sniffs.

"No mate, we're new to the neighborhood. Heck, the whole country to tell you the truth. I'm Frank, he's Max, and this is Dingo Dave."

"Well Dave, I'm sorry to be blunt, but if any babies go missing in the neighborhood, I'm afraid you'll be the number one suspect." Cody joked.

All the dogs laughed and Dave licked his chops lightly.

"Frank, do you mind me asking what kind of dog you are?" Cody asked. "Nice accent by the way."

"Thanks mate. I'm a hot dog in the summer and a chili dog in the winter." Frank sassed. The dogs all grinned.

"I'm a Catahoula Leopard Hound - Australian Shepherd mix. I'm actually from Down Under, but you can find a lot of us down south right here in America, in Louisiana especially." Frank said.

"And Max, I don't think I've ever seen a dog with a bluish-grey coat before. Very cool." Cody said.

"Thanks, I'm a Blue Heeler, an Australian Cattle Dog." Max replied, the red bandana around his neck tied with a single knot.

"How about that. So all of you are from Down Under then?"

"Right. We got sick of all those crazy car chases." Max barked.

"And eating Vegemite kibble all the time was no picnic either." Dave added.

"We needed a change of scenery, and a real gritty adventure we could sink our teeth into." Frank said. "Herding and droving and droving and herding gets a bit stale after a while."

"You just might be in the right place then. Nice to meet you all. Thanks for coming." Cody barked.

Running into the backyard next were Maisey the German shepherd, Kewt the Shiba Inu, Copper the Siberian husky, and Gage the Doberman pinscher. Soon after, Mister Sparky the Pug, zipped in with Fibbledip, a Boston terrier, close on his tail. Buford, a Bloodhound, wandered in next with Skip, a Jack Russell terrier, catching a ride on his back.

"Hey Buford! How you doing?" Maisey asked.

The Bloodhound only shrugged, "Meh, you know, same old-same old: groaking and fetching and fetching and groaking."

The German shepherd's eyes widened slightly as she nodded, "I know how that goes; Table Scrap Patrol can be really stressful. Try nipping their boney ankles next time, it can be pretty effective actually."

Buford smiled and winked at her.

Spatchcock slowly walked into the yard and kept in the back row. A large shadow enveloped him which was strange since he didn't remember seeing any clouds in the sky earlier.

"How you doing little buddy?" Turk asked, his massive body almost blocking out the sun.

"Pretty good big fella." the Chihuahua said with a nod.

"If you need me to lift you up for a better view, feel free to ask." the Newfoundland offered.

"I'm good right down here, but thanks." Spatch said.

A crazy Corgi named Paczki fell out of one of the back yard's trees.

"Yippee!"

All the other dogs looked at him in bewilderment. Clammy, an extra-spotty Dalmatian and Dozer, a saggy-skinned Mastiff ran in, blurting out, "We're here!"

"Good to see you here!" Samson, a Bernese Mountain dog exclaimed.

"Rock on!" Nanner, an Afghan Hound chimed in.

Slabfork, a big burly St. Bernard, gave a slobbery smile.

With Roxie, a Rottweiler, trotting in with Runt, a Weimaraner puppy riding on her back, the meeting was becoming so well-attended, that soon tails were poking out of the chain-link fence.

Maisey felt a tug from behind and looked down to see little Runt pulling her tail, "What's he doing?" he asked, pointing to Smokey, who was licking himself.

"Uhh...I think he's taking a selfie." she answered, trying to conceal the awkwardness of it all.

Last, but certainly not least, Baroo arrived, puffing for breath.

"I...I did...I did my best...rounding up the troops." Baroo wheezed.

"Stellar job, my friend." Cody complimented him.

Baroo wagged his tail and then joined the rest of the pack huddled in front of the porch.

Cody stood proud on the steps, overlooking Timberton's beautiful diversity of dogs. The turn-out exceeded his expectations and the potential here was *paw-some*. Clearly together they would become a formidable force to be reckoned with.

*We know what really matters unlike our so-called dingbat masters.* He sighed and winced a little, not wanting to come down so hard on humans, even though so many of them seemed to enjoy the wanton destruction of their own home.

*They aren't all bad, in fact, many are quite good.*

A quick vision of that kooky dude (Mr. Caldwell?) speeding down a hill in a runaway shopping cart – his tongue flapping in the wind – ran through his mind.

*And some...well...some are just mediocre at best.*

Cody loudly cleared his throat.

"Hey everybody, this isn't a backyard barbeque, so ditch the shorts and flip-flops. This is a mission of utmost importance so please let me have your undivided attention as I break it down."

All the dogs – naked as usual – looked at each other, shrugged, and then turned back to Cody.

"We know what the humans have forgotten." Cody said. "We know the value of having clean water to drink, of having clean soil to dig and bury our bones in, and of having fresh air to breath."

All the dogs nodded in agreement.

"These are gifts from Mother Nature." Cody declared with humility. "We are Dogs, which means we are *LOVE* my friends, and not just any kind of love either. Now tell me brothers and sisters, just what kind of love are we?"

"UNCONDITIONAL LOVE!" the dogs all barked back in unison.

"That's right!" Cody barked. "And we are known for this most precious commodity in the entire universe: Unconditional Love. And we have it in abundance. Being dogs, we have unconditional love for both Mother Nature and Our People. And we will protect OUR PEOPLE from themselves if need be. What they have forgotten - *or have been tempted to forget* - we will make it our mission to remind them."

"Does that mean we will have to disobey them?" Paczki asked.

"We can choose to disobey them if they're in danger of hurting themselves. Sometimes when they're utterly lost we have no choice *but* to disobey them. Tough love isn't easy, but we're willing to go the distance. We can guide them to the right path and bring them back down to earth. For many of them that crucial bond is broken, but we can help heal those wounds. We are also known for Our Loyalty, Our Companionship, and..."

"Teddy bear-thrashing!" Fibbledip shouted. Everybody laughed at this, including Cody.

"Now, as we know, *some* of the humans in attendance tonight are going to be covetous morons who don't care at all about the environment."

"Not more of *those.*"

"Yes," Cody lamented, "more of those."

"We can't let those lame-oh humans spoil it for the rest of us." Cooper spoke up.

"That's right," Cody said. "Fouling the earth with fracking and potentially contaminating our water supply doesn't even register with these numbskulls. Instant gratification of so-called "easy money" is sadly more appealing to them then sustaining a healthy environment. Well, we might not change their minds, *but then again, we just might.* Tonight, when that festering void Chinny Finster is trying to sell the town a raw deal, we will counterattack his propaganda with our own. He'll be standing up for profit and we'll be standing up for NATURE."

"How so?" Skip barked.

"Finster's MO will be predictable no doubt. He'll employ euphemistic language to soften the blows of his misinformation campaign, to help bring their guards down and lull them into a false sense of security. This will be just before he'll present them with the base lure of the "untold fortunes" they'll make if they sign the contracts. While he's hustling the townspeople into accepting fracking, we're gonna crash his party with a little improv A/V presentation of our own."

The dogs howled their approval and wagged their tails.

"And they say you can't teach an old dog new tricks!" Cooper barked.

Cody smiled and scratched behind his ear. "Like I said earlier, the greedy ones will probably be a lost cause, but the ones who are hesitant, and want more information, will be our main targets. See, some people just want money. And others want truth, and we're gonna give it to them."

The sun came out from behind some clouds and a breeze blew over them.

"Now here's what we're gonna do." Cody barked.

Chapter 8

# A Razzmatazzy Town Meeting

IT WAS WITH a mixture of sheer wonder and outright suspicion which Aunt Vivian viewed the interior of the town hall that night. Usually bland and utilitarian, tonight it was decked out with a whole slew of garish adornments including a large spinning disco ball. Golden banners emblazoned with "LET'S GET FRACKING FRIENDS!" were festooned across the dingy green walls.

She had intentionally left Cody in the dark as to her whereabouts, not wanting to disappoint her long-time furry friend. Curiosity had gotten the best of her, yet upon looking around, she was already having second thoughts.

To the right was a long refreshment table, absolutely brimming over with cookies, candy, and pop. Showcased on it stood a large chocolate fountain in the shape of a gushing oil well. Guests dunked and dipped pretzels, marshmallows, strawberries, and even bare fingers into the simply scrumptious chocolatey ooze. Most of the Timbertonians partook of the free "frack snacks." Others, including Viv, avoided them altogether and simply found their seats.

Mister Sparky reached out from underneath the table cloth to snatch a fallen pretzel. He quickly ducked back out of view upon hearing the CLACK CLACK CLACK of some loud heels approaching.

"Mmmmm, these cookies are just flat-out nommy," June Tecklemeyer exclaimed. Barney Wilcox overheard her and reached in to grab a cookie. June quickly slapped his hand away, hissing at him.

"MINE, Sssssssss...." she greedily mumbled through a mouthful of cookies, blowing soggy crumbs everywhere. She glared at him reproachfully as she opened her purse wide and swept the rest of the cookies inside with a bizarre proprietary firmness. She then lifted the purse right up to Barney's face and worked it like a bizarre puppet, opening and closing it like a giant mouth.

"*What's wrong Barney? Didn't get any cookies? That's too bad because they weren't only deeeeeelicious, they were scrumdilly-umptousss!* HA-HA-HA!!" June loudly snapped the purse closed after having the last laugh.

"Wow June! Don't you think everybody deserves at least one cookie?' Barney said.

"No I don't. I think *take-what-you-want* and **to-hell** with everybody else. I also think this Finster guy might have something really worth listening to." June snapped right back at him. "He has oodles of money to offer us I've heard. And I just happen to be in the market."

"I don't know if the money would be worth all the damage fracking might do to the..." he said.

"*You sniveling little coward.* You have a once-in-a-lifetime opportunity to make some real bank and all of a sudden you have to put on a 'concern show' about the environment. Well I care about what's green too! And it's called *MONEY*." She then sneered at him and went to find a seat.

Barney scowled and huffed and puffed, irate from both cookie-deprivation and June's cruel taunts. *That Tecklemeyer is a Tecklemonster.* Barney thought. Counting to ten several times (and backwards once), he finally sighed and went to find a seat.

Hidden underneath a seat, Spatchcock peeked out to see Mister Sparky chewing on something from the refreshment table. His eyes scanned up and over the tablecloth, onto the strawberries and pretzels, and then up and up to the very tippy-top of the chocolate fountain. Rivers of chocolate cascaded down its slippery sides, down, *way down* to the floor. Spatch then wavered on his paws for a moment, struck with lightheadedness. He sat down to wait out the spell.

Meanwhile, Chinny Finster prepped himself for the BIG SELL. Tucked away in the bathroom, he splashed water on his face and grunted at himself in the mirror. He liberally applied cherry beeswax to his big fat pucker and smacked his lips loudly. Sucking in a quick gasp of air, he shifted his tubby bulk slightly to the left as he cut a loud sputtering fart. Sighing relief, he vaguely wondered if he had skid mark insurance.

*Could it really have been a shart?*

That would have to wait though, for now he was revving up for business. The bottom line was MONEY and that would be the only consideration ever to enter his one-track mind. He was so fiendishly delighted with himself, he plunged forward so his belly filled the sink and he could lick and kiss his own horrid reflection in the mirror...which shattered upon the first vile smootch. His tiny limbs flailed wildly about his waterbed tubbiness as he began to snort and heave like an unruly beast while daydreaming of swimming through pools of cold cash.

Back out in the foyer Chinny's flunkies, Bilge Conners, Gretchen Wagglemeister, and Melvin Schramm greeted the guests and directed them to their seats. Alone, each was merely smelly. Together they were just flat-out rank. The artificial mustard-yellow flowers attached to their lapels emitted cheap air fresheners. Regardless, the guests they encountered flared their nostrils in rapt disgust before hurrying off. The dogs had flaring nostrils too, such was the putrid stench of mendacity all around them.

Finally, the town meeting began, a swelling of trumpets announcing Chinny's arrival. Melvin belched out a puff of cruddy confetti. Some of the Timbertonian citizens clapped, others sat unimpressed with their arms tightly crossed over their chests, and a few just slumped over in the lull of sugar comas, chocolate-oil smeared over their needy-greedy little pie holes.

"Thank-you! Thank-you all for attending tonight's special town meeting. As some of you might already know, I'm Chinny Finster, Executive Manager of Leasing for Chesapuke NRG. For tonight's presentation, I want to extend to each and every one of you the opportunity of a lifetime. First of all, I want to take a moment to familiarize you with hydraulic fracking and all of its benefits."

Chinny was a seasoned pro and with his forked tongue – and an incredibly deceptive sleight-of-hand – he began to extol the non-existent virtues of fracking. See Finster was a sly old fox who had ups and downs, and more than just a few all-arounds. Money was what he offered and an abundance of it. But the *cost* was something he never addressed, and what a cost it was!

Yet, unbeknownst to this manipulative maestro as he spewed his hollow offer, lurked some I-Double-Dog-Dare-You type of dogs. They had decided well in advance this whole bogus occasion was a party they just *had* to crash. They had some imperative information to disseminate, but would only succeed if they stuck to their plan with airtight precision and stone-cold conviction. With their stout hearts and twitching tails, the PLAN was a-go.

"...point is THERE IS MONEY TO BE MADE. *Real money.* Your land could be a goldmine, your mineral rights potentially worth thousands of dollars. So why not sign up to have an appraisal expert come out to inspect your property today? Together we could be DIGGING FOR DOLLARS!" Chinny spewed forth, nodding his head continuously throughout his proposal so as to constantly reinforce a false positive.

Smokey crawled under the lovely stinky seats of the audience, getting closer and closer to his target. Being a chew-aholic dog, Smokes was mighty tempted to stop and taste the wad of old green gum stuck under Mr. Muldoonie's chair. Fortunately, Smokes tenaciously stuck to his mission and crawled on. Finally there, he nipped the ankle of Gerald Burkely, signaling him to stand up.

With his ashy complexion mottled with sores, Burkely was a grim figure who stood out in this crowd. As he stood up, Chinny stopped to quickly address him, "Ah sir, we'll have time for questions later on..."

Chinny's mic went dead right on the spot, while simultaneously a little lavalier microphone pinned to Burkely's lapel popped on. He tapped it to make sure, "BUMP-BUMP."

In the backroom's studio, some motley mutts had taken over the control panel. After removing the squirrelly tech-geek Abner from the equation - who was now tied up and gagged in a corner – the mutts fell into Production Mode. Abner didn't mind so much though, as he stayed up most of the previous night watching cheesy animal-attack TV shows and now slept soundly through most of the table-turning. Dozer and Clammy ran their paws over the console, drowning out Chinny's signal to a big fat ZILCH while jacking up Randall's to the max.

"Ladies and gentlemen, if I may have your attention for just a few moments. My name is Gerald Burkely and I'm here to lend some *perspective* to tonight's presentation. I'm from Pennsylvania which many of you know has been ravaged by fracking. I'm putting my neck out on the line tonight even talking to you all. For you see, what Mr. Finster isn't telling you is just how huge the cost of fracking is. IF – and I really hope you don't – sign a lease to allow fracking on your land you will have to sign a non-disclosure agreement first."

"You mean a gag-order?" a concerned citizen asked.

"Exactly. This is how the natural gas industry *slows* the spread of information, especially since *bad news* has a tendency to spread like wildfire. These gag orders are a very strategic part of their damage control, keeping the public ignorant for as long as possible. I'm here tonight to hope you will learn from my own mistakes."

"Is it true fracking can contaminate both water and air?" Barney asked.

"Unfortunately that is true." Gerald answered. "More and more fracking sites have been found to have increased emissions of volatile organic compounds (VOCs) such as benzene, formaldehyde, and toluene. These toxic air pollutants can cause cancer as well as respiratory and neurological harm. And that's not even getting into the massive amounts of methane leakage from most of the wells. Methane of course, is a notorious greenhouse gas which traps heat in our atmosphere which in turn causes global warming. That along with our continued burning of fossil fuels – which creates carbon dioxide emissions – is causing severe damage to our environment."

"Fracking wastewater's a pretty nasty stew I've heard." Another citizen commented.

"You've heard correctly mam. Arsenic, thallium, ammonium, iodide, hydrochloric acid and of course methane are just some of the toxic chemicals found in fracking wastewater, which have a nasty habit of contaminating water-supply wells."

"What effects do these chemicals have on people?" she asked.

"Dizziness, nosebleeds, a higher rate of infant mortality from pregnant women who have breathed the air from areas of fracking activity," he paused, bringing his hand up to his own face. "And skin conditions too."

Vivian's eyes widened as she became woke and anger grew deep inside her heart.

"There's no cause to get shaken up over all this nonsense he's spewing." Chinny tried to yell over Gerald's voice.

"Speaking of shaking, there is also increasing geological evidence that injecting fracking wastewater into deep underground disposal wells can induce earthquakes and other such seismic activity. Oklahoma, once pretty rock-solid, is now more shaky than a natural gas company's version of the truth." Gerald nodded at Chinny, throwing him a contemptuous smile too.

"We have the mineral rights to our property and have the right to sell leases on it!" June Tecklemeyer snapped at him.

"That's true," Gerald agreed. "But you also have the right to all the consequences from such a nearsighted decision."

"*SUCH AS?*" she barked.

"The value of your property can plummet by up to 75%. On top of that, since fracking is an unsustainable business model – that's losing millions of dollars all the time – the gas companies typically shift losses/costs to the landowners, that would be *you*. And then you'll see your royalty payments shrink and shrink while your property is rendered nearly worthless in the long run. And don't forget, most insurance companies consider drilling a hazardous violation of terms and thus you'll most likely encounter trouble there too."

"Are you done yet?" June said, sighing in forced boredom.

Meanwhile, Bilge and Gretchen hurried back to the studio to find out who or what was botching up Chinny's sordid presentation. Bilge grumbled as he found the door to the studio locked.

"Where'd you put the key goofball?" Gretchen seethed.

"You're the one who had it last!" Bilge said.

They began to try to break the door down. Inside the studio, Clammy heard the loud thumps against the door. He tapped his whisker mic.

"Roxie, come in Roxie. This is Clammy from Canine-Control. Are you there?"

After a moment, a loud RUFF was heard, "Yes, this is Roxie, what's up Clammy-Rammy-Ding-Dong?"

"We got two of Chinny's nasty pig henchmen trying to barge into the studio right now and seize operations. This is *not* acceptable. Proceed with Plan C." Clammy commanded.

"We're on it." Roxie barked back.

One after the other, the dogs jumped into the fray until a gigantic dognado of fur and paws swept down the hall, heading straight for the two lumpy henchmen.

"Find an alternate entrance!" Gretchen yelled.

"Why?" Bilge said.

"Because we're about to be shredded wheat, sewer-snout!" she screamed as she began booking down the hall, huffing and puffing like a brazen gorilla. With tattered pant legs and scratched-up shins, the two lugs just managed to jump into the janitor's closet, barricading the door shut. Slabfork immediately laid down in front of it, to make sure the trouble-makers would stay put.

> Chinny was livid as his voice had been muted by those rotten mutts.
>
> *Could things get any worse?*
>
> "My home is now technically a sacrifice zone."

Just then a projected image of Gerald's devastated town appeared on the wall above and behind Chinny's head. The earthquakes, fire water, skin sores, and dismal stats were all on visual display for the audience. Chinny yelled for Melvin to shut down the projection – which was coming from a portable digital projector strapped to the back of Sampson, the Bernese Mountain Dog.

A frisky clutch of smaller dogs: Juju, Morrison, and Mister Sparky ran interference to keep Melvin away just long enough for their presentation to conclude. They circled around the big galoot's ankles in a spinning dervish, making him trip and fall.

"TIMBER!" Juju barked, as Schramm keeled over.

Melvin hit floor with a loud THUD, right in front of the "frackalicious" refreshment table. When he tried to get up, all the dogs took turns biting and tugging on both his shirt sleeves and pant cuffs so that he couldn't. Mister Sparky – nimble as ever – dashed out from underneath the table and quickly managed to attach a leash to one of Melvin's belt loops on his pants.

Not realizing the other end of the leash was attached to the table, Melvin tried to stand up, but instead wound up yanking the refreshment stand's table cloth. The chocolate fountain splashed down on Melvin, creating a sort of mud monster.

Sampson kept a furtive eye out for Melvin, doing his best to keep as still and steady as he could. At least until the video was done. To Sampson's credit, none of the audience members ever wished they had had some Dramamine. The four minute video ran smoothly from the strong and steady perch of Sampson's back. Chinny's hulky frame began to shadow over him just then, making it an ideal time to skedaddle. Which he did along with the smaller dogs. His gig as a portable A/V pooch was over-Rover.

Chinny grabbed slimy Melvin up from the floor, furious.

"Way to go Schramm. You've just let these rotten mutts ruin our presentation. Here's the deal: *YOU* round up ALL of these instigating fleabags and "lose" them somewhere far, far away where they can't interfere with my plans anymore, OR I'll "lose" YOU...permanently. Understand?"

Melvin gulped in fear. "Yes Mr. Finster, I understand completely. Consider it done. Those dogs' tampering days are numbered."

"Get it done." Chinny ordered, letting Melvin drop back down to the floor with a loud SPLAT! Chinny then became keenly aware of just how loud the silence was around him. Looking up, he saw all eyes on him. The audience regarded him with a brooding mixture of incredulity, disgust, and confusion. Chinny knew he had to think fast and the old flimflam huckster in him seized the moment.

"*TAH-DAH!*" he yelled as he spread out his arms wide as if he'd just performed an impressive magic act. "Can I have a round of applause for the Timbertonian Show Dogs!?"

A mild smattering of applause followed.

Vivian, clearly having had enough, stood up, "Sooo...*what?* You're actually saying this whole ruckus was *planned?*"

Cody smiled from underneath a table, keeping a low profile.

"Of course! We wanted to present a town meeting no one would forget in a long time." Chinny fibbed.

"So then, what's the message here? You started out very PRO-fracking, but then the "show" dogs seemed to have contradicted all of that by pointing out – what appeared to me – to be the very dire consequences of fracking." Viv stated, very incredulous now.

Cody's tail thumped with pride.

"Yes, yes! That's what we called the "puppaganda" segment of our show. Fracking is perfectly safe; we were only using the dogs to satirize all of the overzealous environmentalists who falsely try to sway public opinion." Chinny lied through his grimy teeth.

A loud HMM...could be heard from several other skeptical audience members. Unfortunately some of the dimmer ones simply nodded their heads in agreement, buying Chinny's bag of lies lock, stock and barrel. Still, many in attendance could smell the deceit coming off of Chinny Finster like fresh skunk roadkill. Vivian just shook her head in disgust, got up, and left.

"Well, that's quite a clash of communication you've presented to us Mr. Finster." said Rayna Hinson, another audience member with a stern demeanor. "Could you please tell us why you chose to create so much confusion?"

"Entertainment of course!" Chinny quipped. "Everybody knows how boring and stuffy these sort of meetings can be. So we decided to spice it up with a real show!"

"*I'm sure.*" Rayna said. "We have so many alternative sources of *green* energy, including geothermal heat pumps, HVAC systems, fuel cells, small wind energy systems, solar energy systems, solar water heaters, etc. Fracking is just another unregulated money-grab that wreaks irreparable harm on our environment. So you won't be getting *my* land for fracking, I can tell you that much. But thanks for the "frack snacks." She sarcastically made little quotation mark gestures in the air with her index and middle fingers.

Others cited more examples to back up the dogs' claims. Chinny didn't like the independent thinking going on around him and - now with a bullhorn – reemphasized all the money to be made from leasing their land to Chesapuke NRG. Despite this base lure, many people there regarded him with justified disdain and walked out.

Barney Wilcox was just leaving when the puddle of mud-like chocolate on the floor caught his eye. Squatting down, he reached out his right hand and slightly waved it over the muck. Then he tightly pressed the index and middle fingers together and began to erase a large smeared "D." Within seconds he had cleared away another ten letters on the floor, spelling out the truth in the chocolatey goop:

*DIRTY ENERGY*

*Illustration by T.L. Stickle*

As the door slammed shut, Chinny found himself alone in the town hall. He looked scornfully down at the two words scrawled on the floor and growled. The overwhelming consensus had become clear: Timbertonians were against fracking. He then foolheartedly tried to swipe away the words by skidding his foot across them, but wound up slipping and falling into the mud.

Piping mad, Chinny brewed over with fresh anger, all his effort having proved futile. These rubes weren't as easily hornswoggled as he'd hoped. Clearly, he would now need to resort to more drastic (and nefarious) measures. His rubbery mouth tightened up in the corners, forming itself into a ghastly reptilian grin. Slowly, his warty purple tongue slathered across his large mouth, frosting his bruised flabby lips with acidic spit.

In the corner of his eye, he spotted some pretzels scattered about. He crawled through the mud before one of his corny claws seized the snack right off the floor and popped it in his gob.

## Chapter 9

# A Tub of Schramm

MELVIN SCHRAMM WAS in a jam *and* a tub. He had to round up all of those nosey rotten mutts like yesterday. Either that or Finster would have his head (twenty pounds of ugly fat) mounted on a wall; or at least kept in an old economy-sized pickled egg jar filled with formaldehyde (and a sprig of mint).

He was an experienced dogcatcher, but not for dogs like these.

*Not like these.*

These dogs were above his pay grade. These dogs were coordinated and knew how to break formation with evasive maneuvering. Melvin wasn't sure whether or not these dogs might actually be *ninja-dogs*, but they had to be close. These dogs were cray-cray and on the verge of utter chaos. Catching them altogether as one large group would be next to impossible, no matter how squeaky the toys or tasty the treats.

Speaking of treats, Melvin was so disheartened by all the treachery he was responsible for, he didn't even want any of his circus peanuts, which made a spongy light-orange train all around the rim of the tub. Poor wretched troll couldn't even bring himself to gobble the caboose.

*What to do? How can I pull this off?* Melvin thought as he washed the chocolate off his face and out of his greasy hair with some slimy green apple shampoo. The muddy tub water shimmered around the heaving island of his gut. Out yonder from there were the two smaller stubby islands of his knobby knees. A putrid glob of large bubbles erupted from between the islands like a belching swamp.

*Those underwater volcanoes can be quite deadly.* Melvin thought, chuckling to himself. After kind of forgetting everything and staring aimlessly out into space for a spell, he happened to look over at his rubber ducky who sat on the side of the tub in a nest of dirty suds.

"What should I do Mr. Quacky?" Melvin asked with more than a little desperation in his voice. "If I don't round up that canine posse A-S-A-P, then Finster will fire me, and that's just for starters!"

The toy duck just sat there with its wide blank eyes and smiling bill.

"Come on Quacky!" Melvin whimpered, "This is not the time for the silent treatment. I can't get fired! Being a dog-catching henchman is all I know how to do." The slob sat sulking in his suds, severely sourpussed.

*Whatsthat? Whatsthat?*

Through the scratchy screen of his window and deep into the night he heard the low drone of a train whistle somewhere in the background. Melvin stuck a fat finger in one of his ears as if to unplug a cork of wax. It was strange. The whistle – headed southbound from the sound of it – died down, yet the chugging of an old steam engine seemed to grow louder.

The tub began to rattle on the linoleum; the curtains started blowing from their rods, and his fat jiggled like dino-jello as the massive locomotive's cow catcher drove straight over him, hauling endless railroad cars around and around...

*...the rim of his tub!*

*Illustration by T.L. Stickle*

Aye. The circus peanut train was running circles around the rim of Melvin's bathtub, miraculously balanced on the trackless teal porcelain. Little bails of cotton candy steam puffed from its smoke stack. Unbeknownst to Schramm, giant tentacles of tracks rose up all around him, unfurling vertigo-inducing drops and loops along with razor sharp twists and turns.

The little choo-choo slowed down, finally coming to a stop as a loud tea kettle whistle marked its arrival. Through clouds of engine steam, Melvin's eyes widened as if hellzapoppin'.

*"ALL ABOARD!"*

Then (and only then) the toy duck slowly unfurled its usually tucked-in manufacturer's molded wings, strings of hot melted yellow plastic oozing from the hollow feathers. Its little orange feet began to waddle about until the duck stood tall(ish), its cloven eyes shiny, black and doll-like.

"Oh I don't know what to do, I'm Melvy Schrammypoo and my brains are like doggy-doo," Quacky quacked with mock-fret. Kicking a circus peanut overboard for good measure, he pulled a conductor's hat over his little feathered head and checked his pocket watch.

"You weren't born a schlemiel..."Quacky said.

"That's right! It took a whole lotta practice." Melvin agreed.

"Hey Dingleberry Jones, guess what?"

"Whut?" Melvin grunted like an ape.

"You get to ride the *AGITPROP DROP* today!"

"Dah whut?"

Suddenly an over-the-shoulder restraint slammed down tight over Schramm, locking him into his tub.

"*What duh heck?*" Melvin exclaimed.

"Can I borrow one of your fingers real quick?" Quacky asked as he chopped the tip off his stogie with his cigar cutter.

Melvin swallowed hard.

"Just kidding! Now that you're locked in, we can let the fun begin."

Quacky held the GO!-lever in his wingy-hands, edging Mel closer to takeoff: "Keep your arms, legs, and fat ugly head in the car at all times and remember..." the duck advised as he lit a match. The circus peanut train's cow catcher just then burrowed into Melvin's fat head.

"Uhhhh?" Melvin groaned.

"Enjoy your day here at PLAN-LAND, *the Abusement Park!*"

Schramm's tub swiftly ascended a mountainous hill easily twenty-three thousand feet tall as a catchy electro-beat blared from his tub-car's speaker.

"ahem..."

Blowing smoke out, Quacky now pressed his bill up against the microphone and sang:

> *"Up and Up and Up We Go!*
> *By the Time this Ride's Over*
> *You'll have ALL Your Ducks in a Row.*
> *Who Cares What the Future May Bring*
> *We're Ready to Reap What We Sow!"*

*Illustration by T.L. Stickle*

Schramm screamed his ever-loving lungs out as the sudden drop sucked his eyeballs into the back of his (fairly empty) skull. The tub then made a jerky sharp left – sloshing suds off like a foamy root beer - heading for a series of loops.

*"Now Legally We Can Make Them Dizzy*
*And YES! We Can Make Them Sick*
*And If They Complain Too Loud*
*The Pollies We Purchased*
*Know Just the Trick...*
*To Prevent Any Public Uprising*
*With Some Cheap On-Camera Sympathizing*
*We'll Promise Things Will Change*
*-With an Ever-Elusive "WHEN"-*
*Then Laugh Behind Closed Doors*
*And Just Go Ahead & Do It AGAIN!"*

Upon violently spinning upside down seven times, Melvin blew chunks all over himself, the coaster-tub, and Quacky. The rubber duck shook some puke off his umbrella, giving Melvin a look of disgust. Another formidable hill up ahead found the duck crooning like a seasoned pro:

*"My Head is Hollow and I've Got*
*More Brains than You*
*For Smarts You've Got Bupkis*
*From All That Time Wasted*
*Living in the Human Zoo."*

The tub-coaster zigzagged into a dark tunnel, which suddenly lit up with spiraling strobe lights as the melty duck capped off his tune with real panache.

*"Let's Milk This Mudball for All it's Worth*
*Drill Out the Guts of Mother Earth*
*We'll Never Allow Mere Science to Stand in Our Way*
*The Only Thing That Really Matters*
*Is What Big Oil & Gas Have to Say"*

Melvin barfed all over the side of the tub (again) and then swished some tub water in his mouth and spat as the car came to a screeching halt.

"Okay, you took me to 'Plan-Land' and belted out a cool song and everything...but...what *is* the plan anyway?"

Quacky only sighed as he packed up his conductor's hat and galoshes into his green suitcase.

"Use the Cody-dog as bait to nab the other mutts. *Yadda-Yadda-Yadda.*"

"BRILLIANT!" Schramm squealed.

"I have to be moving on to my next gig, some venue up in ..."

"*Whut?*"

"I said...ahem...I HAVE TO BE MOVING ON...."

"WHUT?!" Melvin scratched his rat's nest as if trying to stimulate

some thought up there. Next the slobbasaurus blew the last two (snot-dipped) circus peanuts out of his schnozzola, somehow "thinking" that would improve his hearing.

*Illustration by T.L. Stickle*

"Greasy galoot." Quacky fussed at the lout as he used his little pink plastic spoon to shovel out some of the chunky caramel-colored wax inside Melvin's ear. Schramm grunted excitedly as he palm-hit the sides of the tub.

Quacky next reached inside his feathers and pulled out a shiny black plastic comb.

"Coom feaderz?" the Schramm blurted in wonderment.

The duck only narrowed his eyes, next removing a small square of wax paper, which he neatly folded over the comb.

"Ahem..." the duck cleared his throat before playing his wax paper comb harmonica with eerie gusto.

The loud buzzing distortion melted all the coaster tentacles, and the train whistled one last time, marking its departure.

*Woooooot-wooooooooo...*

Melvin didn't recognize the tune, but it had a wonderful kazoo-like flavor to it all the same. Upon finishing, Quacky threw the wax paper away and dipped his comb into the wad of Schramm's gooey ear wax.

Humming to himself, he combed his feathered hair back, disheveled no more.

He was one slick duck.

# Chapter 10

# Farmer Redfox's Dark Barn

THE MUZZLE WAS tightly strapped around Cody's head and snout.

"That kept you nice and quiet didn't it?" Melvin teased. "Silence suits you well *dog*." The oafish thug finally removed it, only to quickly stick a dog whistle in his mouth.

"And that suits you well too, doesn't it? You are a whistle-blower after all, aren't you *dog*?"

Cody held it limply, almost letting it drop to the ground. Melvin's meaty hand tightened its grip on his furry shoulder. Cody looked up to see him make a grim slicing gesture across his fat neck.

"Think about Timmy, Mr. Top Dog." Melvin warned.

*Where could he be? I can't do this to my friends. But if I don't, would they really hurt my precious boy? But if I betray my friends, will they forgive me? And could we still be okay somehow?* Cody jumped from thought to thought as a million concerns raced through his mind.

Cody came out of his brainstorm as Melvin quickly snuck a collar over his head, attached to a chain leash.

"What's the big idea?" Cody growled.

"Don't wanna see you running off anywhere." Melvin grunted, giving the leash a good yank, tightening the collar around Cody's neck. "Especially now that we're getting friendly and everything."

"If this is friendly, I'd hate to see what you consider mean."

Melvin smiled a horrible grin, "Not a pretty sight let me tell you."

*I don't really have much of a choice, for Timmy's sake this has to be done..* Cody thought. Feeling something close to hope, his reluctance passed. Through the sides of his snout, he inhaled deeply.

Then he blew the whistle.

Throughout Timberton, a wild assortment of dog ears suddenly perked up upon hearing the high frequency sound. They knew from experience the whistle was *only* used for spur-of-the-moment emergency meetings in which the dogs would all rendezvous at Farmer Redfox's barn, out in the sticks.

In their typical true community spirit, they answered the call immediately and came booking down the boulevard from every nook and cranny around town. They all wondered just what could be wrong.

One by one, the dogs entered the old ramshackle barn to find Cody at the front, ready to begin the meeting. Yet, not one of them could help wonder why Cody was so solemn in greeting them. Even when the problems they would face together were tough, he still greeted them with a strong spirit.

Tonight was different though. Their leader was not the happy and confident chocolate lab they'd known and grown to love. Moreso than usual, they could smell the wood rot of the sunken barn. Cody seemed almost cold and very apprehensive, a certain look in his eyes made all the dogs very uneasy.

When they looked up into the barn's rafters and saw nothing but blackness, that didn't help either. Many of the dogs were coming down with fresh cases of the heebie-jeebies. Usually they heard an occasional hoot (or two) from Gorky the resident barn owl. Tonight nobody gave a hoot.

*Where were the lanterns which usually hung from the walls?* They wondered, confused to see only one lantern up front by Cody, and it was dimly lit, burning low.

*Illustration by T.L. Stickle*

*Why?*

Cody had informed Melvin at least twenty-one dogs would be showing up for this "emergency" meeting. He knew that in reality as many as thirty could show up, but he kept it to himself. If even one dog didn't make it to the meeting on time, then there was a chance. He now counted twenty-one dogs in the barn and knew he wasn't the only one doing the counting.

"Okay, now that we're all in attendance, I would like to commence the meeting." Cody spoke in a glum demeanor.

"What's this all about Cody?" Fibbledip asked.

"Is schomezink wrong vis sose frackink jerks again?" Dagmar said.

"Not anymore." a loud voice from above replied.

All the dogs looked around, but could not find the source of the voice.

Suddenly the barn doors slammed shut, the loud metallic snapping of padlocks quickly following.

"Forgive me." Cody said.

Heavy rope nets flung down on them from above. Within seconds they were all trapped and barking frantically.

"Jumpin' Jehoshaphat!" Cooper said.

"Fat Joe's got nothing to do with this." Maisey replied.

Melvin Schramm then walked up front behind Cody, now wearing a gas mask. Next he reached into his pockets and withdrew two large orange balls with little black zigzags running through their middles. Each had a blue button on it.

"Now sleep. *Sleep*, you rotten mutts." Melvin cooed.

He pressed the buttons and the fizzy rush of pink gas immediately shot out of the balls, which he tossed toward the dogs.

"You didn't fall into the trap so much as you ran into it with arms wide open," the slovenly henchman sneered. "Next time try listening to your instincts."

*Why don't I ever do that?* he thought to himself.

The sedative fumes were powerful and within seconds their loud barking diminished to nothing more than a few random yelps. After a minute, silence.

"Get the van." Melvin spoke into a Walkie-talkie.

-

"In this case, better never than late." Clover said.

"You got that right." Spatchcock said.

Both dogs had only caught the tail-end of the dog whistle. When they had almost reached the barn, they spied two shadowy figures slamming the doors shut and locking them up tight, at which point they quickly ducked out of sight.

"With these stupid mongrels out of the way, torching the orchards will be a cinch." One of the shadows said.

"We're still set for tomorrow then?" the other shadow asked.

"Six o'clock on the nose. It's Sunday and nobody will be there." The first shadow replied. He then grabbed something off his belt and raised it to his face.

"Be there in a jiff." He answered, then walked off to a large vehicle parked nearby.

"Where you going?" the second shadow asked.

"You heard the Schramm, let's go get the van." The first said.

Spatchcock and Clover stayed low to the ground, their eyes now wide with shock.

"Did you hear that?" Clover said.

"I can't believe it, but yes, I did hear it." Spatch replied. "*Now what?*" Clover said, but before Spatch had time to reply, the low rumbling of the van could be heard as it parked right in front of the barn. To both dogs' dismay, they watched as the henchmen dragged the nets full of their friends into the back of the van.

"Where are they taking them?" Clover said.

"I have no idea." Spatch answered.

"Maybe we should follow them."

"Then we'd get caught too." Spatch said. "No, we need to tap into some other local resources. This job is way too big for just the both of us."

"Which job is that? Saving our friends or saving the rumble-barry orchard?" Clover asked.

"Both, but if you think about it, we can only try to save the rumblebarry orchard for now."

"Because we know where the orchard is, but don't have a clue as to where they're taking our friends." Clover spelled it out.

"Exactly. Now what I'm about to suggest is going to sound like sheer lunacy - *and it probably is* - BUT..."

"But?"

"We're clearly desperate at this point and pressed for time and oh, wouldn't you know, we're fresh out of other options too."

"You're not suggesting making some unholy alliance with..."

"*Meow.*"

Spatchcock spoke the ominous word and now, even more than merely suggesting it, both dogs knew it was their destiny.

# Chapter 11

# Chinny Underestimates

"ARSENIC, BENZENE, MANGANESE, methane, yadda-yadda-yadda." Chinny said. "I could care less about their constant gripes about 'contaminated drinking water,' and all the toxic chemicals they keep finding in our fracking fluids."

"But the DOH and EPA could get back to us with enough evidence." Lester Higgins, a lawyer for Cheasapuke NRG said, speaking from the video monitor.

"You don't get it; we have bought them out-ALL OF THEM-completely. Almost every state's Department of Health has now been rendered impotent. They have strict orders NOT to follow through with any complaints related to natural gas drilling. Heck! We NOW force them to abandon their own investigations. Ditto with the EPA. No matter how much evidence accumulates, they are being extremely well paid to look the other way." Chinny laughed as he inserted a large steel needle into the back of his own neck.

"Aren't they a government agency though?" Higgins asked, cringing at the same time.

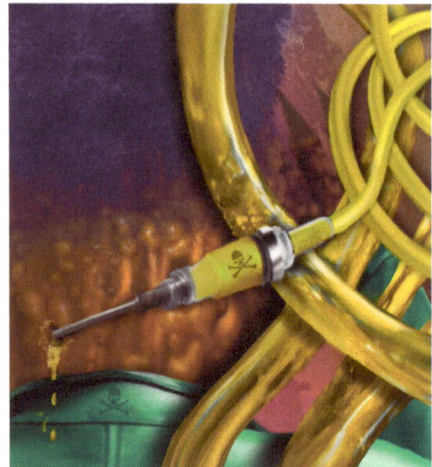

*Illustration by T.L. Stickle*

"So what? That wonderfully money-greedy VP back in the early 2000s made sure there was a huge loophole in the Safe Water Drinking Act didn't he? And now nobody has to report which chemicals are even used in fracking fluid!" Chinny quipped. "Money talks, *NOT* the people. The people are only going to whine and complain, but the others – that's the majority mind you – *will* sell out. And when their "precious" water is no longer fit to drink, we'll sell that to them too!"

A green light blinked three times and the fracking fluid began to surge forward through the thick transparent tubing, pumping a toxic mystery blend of chemicals into Finster. His flabby warts grew engorged and bulbous. One even popped like a mutant zit. He began to grow drowsy listening to the percolating suck-n-breathe of the transfusion machine.

"Can you imagine the sheer amount of money we could make by having weekly water buffalos delivered to these fools?" Chinny slobbered.

"Water buffalos?" Higgins asked.

"Cisterns, water tanks, you know...Nesleaze will be all over that action..." Chinny yawned, and – bloated from a fresh injection of frack juice - sunk right into the sloshing waterbed of his own gelatinous self, drifting off into sweet slumber.

Chapter 12

# Urgent Information

Mote – up in a rumblebarry tree watching the mindless henchmen leave the orchard in a creepy serial killer van - quickly scribbled a note, "*Contact me ASAP: URGENT! – luv Mote*" and stuck it to a walkie talkie with a wad of old blue bubblegum. Setting both radios to channel seven (to make sure they would be on the same frequency) he hoped the 23-mile range would be wide enough to allow communication with Cody.

"I thought you and that dog hated each other?" Ruby said.

"*No way!* We play games together – sometimes very intense games – but we always come back to each other as friends." Mote answered.

"Maybe you're both out there where the buses don't run."

The rat only shrugged then petted Ruby the Jackdaw, letting his little pink claw slide over her silky black feathers. The bird cawed softly. "Ruby, we're all in terrible danger and I need you to fly lightning-fast and deliver this walkie-talkie to Cody."

"Where is he? How will I find him?" Ruby asked.

"I don't know, but if anybody can, it's you. With a bird eye's view - and that he's traveling with an entire pack of dogs - it shouldn't be as difficult as it sounds." Mote answered.

"Easier said than done." Ruby cawed, clicking her talons on the branch.

"I'm sorry Ruby, but I need you to seek from above with fierce intent. Heck, break the sound barrier if you can swing it. Just find Cody." Mote implored the formidable bird.

"For Timberton and its rumblebarries, I will fly with great speed and purpose. Wish me luck." Ruby said as she unfurled her wings, grabbing hold of the sky. Clobber loudly meowed as Mote looked down only to realize he was twisting up little fistfuls of the cat's fur. He quickly relinquished his grip.

"Sorry Clobber, I'm beyond nervous." Mote apologized. "Now, let's get to work. Time is not on our side."

# Chapter 13

# Be Brave In The Cave

A QUIRKY ECHO skipped through the chocolate lab's ears: PLINK!-plink-plink-plink...

*PLINK!-plink-plink-plink...*

Cody opened one of his eyes, blinking several times trying to focus. Wherever he was, it was very dark.

PLINK!-plink-plink-plink...

*What is that? A guinea pig smacking a thimble?* Cody thought.

*Maybe a chicken trying to tune a harp?*

Opening the other eye, the woke canine searched for the source of this mysterious sound. Finally his bright brown eyes rested on a puddle.

PLINK!-plink-plink-plink...went the echo of a drop of water as it hit the puddle. Cody twitched his ears, taking in the strange acoustics of this even stranger place. He gave an investigatory bark which of course echoed right back at him. The other dogs began to awaken from their slumber.

"Where are we?" Smokey asked.

"It looks like a cave," Cody said.

"How dit vee all geten here?" Dagmar said, bewildered.

"And why did we all fall asleep here?" Maisey wondered.

The groggy dogs traded in their yawns and disorientation for fear and concern as they heard the loud fluttering of bat wings above them. They huddled close together in a tight-knit pack. They were in the large mouth of a dark cave, one seemingly full of giant sharp teeth. It was cold, damp, and drafty too.

*Photo Collage by T.L. Stickle*

"Chinny's henchmen knocked us out with sleeping gas and then apparently got us out of the way by stashing us all in this dark creepy cave." Cody explained.

"Out of the way for what?" Cooper asked.

"That's what I'm afraid of." Cody said. "I'm also sad to admit I led you all into the trap over at Farmer Redfox's barn."

"Vy?" Dagmar asked.

"They threatened to harm my boy Timmy if I didn't comply with their orders. It was an awful spot to be in and I'll understand if some of you don't trust me anymore, but I was just trying to do the right..."

Cooper put his paws over Cody's shoulders, looked him dead in the eye and said, *"I knew it was you Fido."*

He looked at all the other dogs huddled together. Not one of them blinked, but all of them smiled and then laughed.

Cody laughed too, "Copy that, Dogfather."

"For real, we understand Cody, and we would've done the same." Cooper said.

"Yeah we got your back pal." Maisey said.

Cody panted some relief. "Thanks gang, your unconditional love is giving me a serious case of the feels."

He then barked loudly into the darkness and listened carefully. His bark bounced back quickly. The other dogs turned their heads from side to side, curious if not confused.

"What are you do...?" Smokey began to ask.

"Shhh," Cody hushed him right up. Next, he turned in the opposite direction and barked loudly once again into the darkness. This time his echo seemed to travel well into the distance, causing the big brown dog to smile.

"There's an echo!" Smokey exclaimed, as something scampering on the ground caught his eye.

"Don't fret; this certainly isn't the first time we've been in an echo chamber. Everybody listen up," Cody said. "We're getting out of here right now. I want everyone to line up behind me single-file and *gently* bite the tail in front of you, until we've formed a chain. Nobody's getting lost on my watch."

All the dogs kind of just stood there, looking at him and then at each other, except for Smokey who was chowing down on a mutant albino cave roach.

*KEEEE-RUNCH!* (The bug's spindly antennae tickled his throat on the way down.)

"Come on!" Cody growled. "What are you waiting for? Arbor Day?"

*Illustration by T.L. Stickle*

The dogs then began to hustle, bumping into one another at first. Eventually they had formed one long furry dog centipede, all bound for the nearest exit.

"Okay gang, we're gonna walk out of here together AS ONE." Cody said. "Please be considerate of each other and DO NOT FART."

This elicited a wave of muffled laughter from the dogs.

"And I'll know too as I have the keenest sense of smell."

Once Maisey had bit down on his tail, Cody hollered, "Take it nice and slow and steady. Pretty sure my super-sniffer can lead us to the nearest exit."

## Chapter 14

# Who Goes There?

"IS THIS THE place?" Clover asked.

They were on Ratford Avenue, but still he had to be absolutely sure, so Spatchcock looked at the establishment on his left:

Bellemew's Theremins (*okay, check*),

then over to the one on his right:

Cosselcoarse's Crossbones Tavern (*okay, check*),

and finally up to the creepy dilapidated building right in front of them: Fat-Cat Chow Factory (*okay, totally check*).

"Ohhh, yes...most definitely."

Clover looked up at the boarded up windows and the heavy chains locking the entrance. "I wouldn't've ever guessed."

"Exactly, no one would." Spatchcock whispered as he approached the door. "Now follow me."

Clover did, and Spatch lead them behind a large cement planter next to the door, where there was a little hole in the wall.

"Hidden passage, *nice*." Clover said as she squeezed through the opening which led into a front section of what once were probably administrative offices. They hadn't tippy-toed more than a few feet when they were quickly apprehended by a behemoth cat guard, who swung out from behind a cubicle wielding two golden sickles.

"Who goes there...*MEOW?!*" the beastly tabby demanded.

"I...I am Spatchcock and this...this is Clover."

"I am Sledge. State your business."

The two nervous dogs explained their predicament; being wise enough to emphasize it was also *the cats'* predicament. Sledge listened, wary of them, as they were dogs and dogs usually had no business here.

"Such collaboration seems unlikely, but I'm not paid to make such decisions. Follow me and keep quiet." Sledge ordered.

They followed the mangy mountain of a cat through dark corridors which eventually brightened. Finally they stopped at a large red oak door, emblazoned with two gilded golden cats scratching at opposite sides of the entrance.

## Chapter 15

# Bumblesquatch The Bear

THE DOG-CENTIPEDE slowly wormed itself out of the mouth of the cave and down a dark, treacherous tunnel. The dogs' eyes darted all around them as they were enshrouded in a cacophony of plinks, high-pitched bat shrieks, and the hoarse whisper of the draft crawling over them. Despite having their mouths full of tails, some of the dogs managed to frown even moreso when they stepped into icy cave puddles.

Suddenly Cody stopped, causing a bit of a doggie pile-up. They had reached a fork in the tunnel, one way reaching out to the left, and the other to the right.

"Sorry everyone, but we now have a decision before us."

"Yuck!" Smokey barked as he spat out Dagmar's tail.

"I'm schure yorz tastes liken lemon kake." Dagmar snapped back at him. (He walked underneath her for the rest of the way.)

Cooper turned back to Nanner, "If you keep yanking my tail like that, you're going to pull it off."

"Don't worry, it'll grow back." Nanner lazily reassured him.

"No it won't. I'm a dog not a lizard."

"My bad."

"What kind of decision?" Smokey spoke up.

"The tunnel has now split off into two directions and I guess we need to decide which way to take." Cody explained.

"How do we do that?" Fibbledip said.

"Well, we're dogs and don't carry coins. Thus, we can't flip one." Cody lamented.

"We could always just flip Smokey, he's just a runt of a dog." some dog quipped in an unrecognizable voice.

"I'll flip *YOU*." Smokey yipped back.

"I guess we could take a vote." Cody said.

"Zat's a goot idea, bekause it schure ain't gettink any varmer in here." Dagmar agreed.

"I really wish there was someone more informed to help us make this decision." Cody fussed.

Suddenly a loud scampering accompanied with a strange sputtering sound could be heard coming from *one* of the tunnels. *But which one?*

The dogs repeatedly turned their heads from right to left as if watching a criss-crossy tennis match, trying to discern from which tunnel the approaching ruckus was coming from.

"LEFT-LEFT!!" half the dogs barked.

"RIGHT-RIGHT!" the other half barked.

*"HAHLA-BALOOOOO!"* a large bear cried as he shot out of the right tunnel, screeching to a halt in front of the dogs, whose eyes widened in fear.

"Ant voo mighten *you* be?" Dagmar asked.

"Uhh, try to remember he's *a bear* Dagmar." Cody urged.

"I'm Bumblesquatch the Bear and don't worry little fella, I'm not a mean bear, but rather *a show-bear!*"

"Sho-bah?" Dagmar said.

In an awkward attempt to dazzle them with his spiffy dancing skills, the lumbering beast put three paws forward and two steps back.

"CHA-CHA-CHA!" he declared.

*Silence.* Even the crickets had decided to bail.

Finally, tiny old Fibbledip approached the bear.

"Uh, Mr. Bumblesquatch?" Fibbledip said.

"Ahhh, YYYYYEEEEEEEESSS?" Bumby enthusiastically responded.

"If you could help lead us out of here, back to the outside world, it would be an impressive accomplishment to add to your résumé."

Bumblesquatch nodded feverishly, especially with the opportunity to help out his fellow creatures. "I would be more than happy to get all of you dogs out of this cave, but first I want to say something to..." Bumblesquatch cut himself off with his own loud fart.

"Ahem...sorry about that. I eat a lot of cabbage, slaw, and all sorts of fermented stuff." Bumblesquatch explained.

"Goot gut health." Dagmar nodded.

As the bear's putrid stench hit the airwaves, the dogs began twitching their snouts from side to side, trying to shake free of the evil air biscuits with extra gravy. In fact, the dogs were struggling to either remain polite so as to escape or just flat-out run away for fresher air.

"Follow me guys and I'll have you out of here in no time." Bumblesquatch said, taking the lead. And just like that he started down the left tunnel.

"Form a chain again everybody!" Cody barked. "We're following Bumblesquatch back to the outside world!"

## Chapter 16

# King Ridley Kat of Yiddlesmeyer

SLEDGE SLOWLY PUSHED open the heavy door, a loud scraping accompanying it. The dogs' eyes widened at the spectacle revealed. The squalid exterior turned out to be a dingy veneer for a throne room of repurposed wonder.

Old spiral conveyor chutes now stood as giant steel candlesticks for recycled tuna can chandeliers and even doubled as joyous corkscrew kitty slides. The ceiling ducts had been painted emerald green and lovingly transformed into an intricate catwalk (for those felines not suffering from acrophobia). Large metallic mixers now regave themselves as cauldrons for gobs of hot cat chow, savory mouse stew, and buzzy catnip. One old mixer – tucked away in a dark corner - was even being used as a hairball spittoon. *Yuck.*

The sweet deep tones of didgeridoo filled the throne room and Clover had had no idea cats could master circular breathing. Strings of yarn in a kaleidoscopic array of colors were festooned about the lively surroundings, whether for play or decoration was hard to say. The cats' eerie glowing eyeshine peeped out at them from everywhere.

"You have arrived in the midst of a gifting ceremony, in which his highness, King Ridley, bestows lavish presents on his most loyal subjects." Sledge explained. The dogs looked at him, mildly befuddled.

"Which means you must wait until he will see you, *IF* he will." Sledge said with a growling purr.

Just then the loud *BRUM-BRUM-BRUM* of drums and the swell of sassy trumpets smothered the didgeridoo music. Straight ahead was a throne flanked by two giant scratching post columns. There sat King Ridley Kat of Yiddlesmeyer, a regal Maine Coon with a ruby-encrusted crown atop his head. The dogs waited to be invited up to speak before the king.

*Illustration by T.L. Stickle*

"My most loyal subjects, you all are to be rewarded today for your fastidious dedication to my kingdom." King Ridley declared. He pressed a button on the armrest of his chair and large panels of flooring slid away in front of the cats, revealing dark square holes. Curious meows could be heard up and down the rows of felines. One of them barfed up a hairball into one of the holes. Ridley just sighed.

"Let the Gifting Ceremony commence!" King Ridley exclaimed. And with another push of the button, large, beautiful wrapped presents rose up out of the floor. The cats were now in a complete tizzy, meowing excitedly as if the nonstop sound of a can opener were grinding through their heads.

The cats quickly shredded the ribbons and bows to tattered confetti, then ripped off the lids to the presents.

Inside the lavish presents were a veritable plethora of kitty goodies: plushy mice dolls to pummel, packs of internationally-blended gourmet catnip, tuna-scented perfume, dog-shaped dart boards (Spatchcock and Clover gulped in unison), and even silk bags full of gold dust kitty litter.

"Well, what do you think of the gifts I've given you?" King Ridley asked. Positively giddy, the cats were grinning from ear to ear and then proceeded to dump out all of the presents, casually discarding them, so they could then jump right into the boxes.

*BOXES!*

Snug and cozy glorious boxes! Irresistible to cats everywhere.

"Cats *is* cats." King Ridley said, shrugging. He pressed the button once again, lowering his box-loving subjects down into the floor, as a snuggly lullaby enveloped them from below.

*"La-la-laaa...bloop-bloop-bloop...bah-nah, bah-nah...boing!"*

The floor panels having slid back into place, he then began to chew and pull on a stretchy snack of rat-tail taffy, spooling it up on a paw like spaghetti on a furry fork.

## Chapter 17

# Corporate Slimeball

FINSTER RIPPED THE needle from his skull, tossed it to the floor, and then screwed the cap back onto the hole in his head, tightening it with one final twist. He then smacked his lips a few times, his appetite increasing.

Higgins did a lousy job of concealing his disgust for Finster's repulsiveness. Chinny didn't notice – and if he had he wouldn't've cared – and only violently shook his head from side to side for a long moment, slobber flying from his slimy gob.

"Sure you're not underestimating them?" Higgins asked. "Sounds to me like you're getting awfully close to pushing them to a breaking point."

"These people are weak and easily distracted. They have no real fight in them. They are bought and sold everyday. And cheaply I might add. A dime a dozen. Do you know what they're going to do? They're not going to do *anything* but exactly what we want them to." Chinny said, spelling out his tainted perception of Timberton. He began to bite off and chow down on his own fingernails.

"I hope you're right Finster."

"I am. I don't care if we frack every single national park in the country. Every stream, every river, every lake, and the garbage-strewn oceans can burn for all I care. We're not interested in crap like that. We're only interested in MONEY. *And lots of it.*" Chinny grunted through his crunching piehole.

"And when we run out of residential leases? What then?"

Chinny tilted his head back as he put his right wrist to his forehead, feigning melodrama, "Oh, what *SHALE* we ever do?"

"Ha-ha." Higgins responded.

"Taking a page right from the former VP's playbook, we can have our highest-ranking *bought* politician go back into negotiations with the BLM to..."

"BLM?" Higgins butted in again, seeking clarification.

"The BLM, the Bureau of Land Management. We can make them dance to our beat once again, and thus gain access to so-called 'public lands' such as mineral-rich national parks and whatnot."

"You make it sound so easy. *Maybe too easy.*"

"If it could be done in 2001, imagine how easy it is now." Chinny gloated as he grabbed another bright red box of crispy fingernails off the shelf. "Especially now that we've nearly quadrupled the amount of flacks shilling for the oil and natural gas industries, spending over seven billion dollars a year for our lobbyists to...*ahem*...persuade our friends in Washington, who in turn are more than happy to subsidize the fossil fuel industry by billions of dollars every year. Trust me, the ROI is magnificent."

Lester laughed with him then asked, "What about that huge lawsuit from the citizens in Pennsylvania? We had destroyed their water supply and they were suing us for the cost of the new waterline right? Over ten million in damages if I'm correct."

*Illustration by T.L. Stickle*

"It would've been." Chinny laughed, placing the new corny claws on his fingertips. "But we were quicker on our feet. We bought the governor for less than two million and like a good lapdog he carried out our agenda to a T."

"How so?" Lester asked, licking his scorched chops in rapt curiosity.

"First we had him kill the waterline, the one that was supposed to connect to the municipal water supply. THEN, we had him repeal moratoriums on fracking throughout the rest of Pennsylvania's state forests and other public lands." Chinny cackled, wiggling his claws in the air.

Lester laughed again, but then wondered, "Their water is now poisoned though! How can we even get away with that legally?"

Chinny then literally fell to the floor and started to roll around on it, bellowing laughter like a hog from hell, "We...we ha...had already bo...bought the EPA too, so we had them declare their water "safe to drink!"

"Nooo!" Lester smirked, giggling at the sheer deviltry of it all.

"YES! The EPA does our bidding even more than DuPont's these days." Finster hollered, laughing so hard, salty tears ran from his eyes like acid from old batteries. "See, you just wait long enough – *and pay off all the right people* – and that revolving door between our government and powerful corporations will spin in our favor too."

"Slick." Higgins commented, clearly impressed with the methods employed.

"Now you'll have to excuse me Lester, but I have to go warm my hands by the fire."

# Chapter 18

# Smelly Escape

THE DOGS QUICKLY made their way down the left tunnel. Cody was nervous they might've actually lost the big old bear. It was pitch dark in there after all and he had no idea just how far ahead Bumblesquatch might've already gone. His concern was quickly alleviated however as he heard a sputtering plum-pudding series of farts not far ahead, the echoes sounding like a barrage of sour trumpet blasts.

"More proof natural gas really stinks." Cody said. He heard Bumbly growl under his breath up ahead.

"Whoever smelt it dealt it." the stinky bear retorted.

"I schmelt it, but I dealt *nosink*." Dagmar declared, flaring her nostrils in rapt disgust.

"Hey Cody, still glad you have the keenest sense of smell?" Smokey cracked.

"Just keep walking." Cody grumbled.

All throughout the arduous journey out of the cave, Cody quickly came to hate three sounds:

1. Loud Whistling
2. Loud Coughing
3. Loud Farting.

Specifically those coming from Bumblesquatch, who very unconvincingly used the first two to cover up his obnoxious farting. His foul odor was so palpable it began to develop an eerie phosphorescent glow, so any attempt to hide it was incredibly futile. On the bright side, being able to actually *see* the bear's farts alerted Cody and the pack to fall back into shallow breathing mode.

*Illustration by T.L. Stickle*

Next the stank-bear tried to divert their attention with some family anecdotes. "Once I gave my cousin Fuzzy some Roraine and he never spoke to me again," he mumbled. "See that's the problem: nobody has a sense of humor anymore."

"He wasn't mad at you forever, wuzzy?" Smokey asked.

"I don't know about all that, but he was pretty peeved." Bumbly replied.

Cody decided it was best to let Bumbly know to cut out the whole charade. "Hey buddy, you need a cough drop up there?"

The bear only farted louder.

"Ooooh! That one has a fruity bouquet." the bear sneered.

This time Cody growled under his breath.

The other dogs were better off smelling each others' butts.

Cody heard the bear's whistling again, signaling another wave of fetid gas. Grimacing, Cody's hackles bristled as he tried to contain his anger.

"What's that tune you're whistling; maybe we can all join in." Cody said. Again, the bear blasted yet more toxic fumes right down into the dogs' air supply, this time actually giggling.

"How uncouth! *EXCUSE YOU!*" the relentlessly gassy bear quipped. "You better be careful Cody, I feel a shart coming on."

Cody's watering eyes widened as it dawned on him it was gradually getting brighter. There was another light source developing besides the fuzzy soft green glow of Bumbly's relentless stink bombs. The jagged surfaces of the cave's walls were slowing gaining definition. There was *daylight* ahead for sure. Cody knew it. With each step (and fart) things became more visible.

"HALT!" Cody yelled. All the dogs stopped and let go of each others' tails. Cody turned to look back at his pack of friends. For the first time in quite a while, he could really see them.

"I've been trying to hold my breath, but I'm on the brink of suffocation. I can't take anymore; in fact my sense of smell might be permanently damaged. So, at the count of three we're all gonna run towards the light and right outside into the fresh air."

All the dogs cheered and booked at two (not even waiting for three), straight out of the tunnel past Bumblesquatch.

"*REALLY!*" Bumblesquatch huffed indignantly.

Needless to say, the dogs – especially Cody – breathed the sweet fresh air deeply, revitalizing themselves. Even though Cody's nostril hairs were singed and slightly smoking when they finally departed the cave, he still managed to thank Bumblesquatch for helping to rescue them.

"Ahhh, 'twernt nothin'." Bumblesquatch said. "Glad I could *so heroically* be of service. Now excuse me, but this here *saint* needs to find another tasty cabbage patch to raid. But I wouldn't...ahem...turn my nose up...to a crunchy kohlrabi or two either." Licking his chops, the big old stinky bear lumbered into the forest, sputtering toots from his furry behind.

"Boy, was that bear ever sassy..." Cooper started
"...oont gassy." Dagmar finished.

*Illustration by T. Stickle*

"Everybody listen up: snouts down, pick up the scent - we need to make some serious tracks." Cody addressed the team.

"Why?" Fibbledip asked. "After all that, we need to rest."

"Don't you see? We don't have *any* time to rest. In fact, we just might be too late already." Cody barked.

"Too late for what?" Mister Sparky asked.

"We are way out in the middle of nowhere, at least twenty miles from Timberton. Why do you think?" Cody asked.

"Bekause zay vanted usch outen oov zee vay." Dagmar said.

"BINGO! *B-I-N-G-O.*"

"So Chinny and his nasty henchmen could do whatever they wanted without any meddling dogs trying to get in his way!" Turk barked.

"Just like when we stuck it to them at the town meeting." Maisey said.

"And whatever they want scares me to death." Cody said. "Now, let's move, my friends, *and fast.*"

The dogs raced through the forest, due north, towards Timberton.

## Chapter 19

# A Little Purr-Suasion

SLEDGE LOUDLY CLEARED his throat, to get King Ridley's attention.

"Now what?" King Ridley said.

"Your Royal Highness, we have two dogs here to see you, with what appears to be a most crucial and urgent message." Sledge explained.

"Very well, show them in."

As they made their way up the aisle to the throne, King Ridley glared at them. He put down his mouse-kabob and stein of cream so as to properly assess these motley mutts. Sledge held his sickles tightly against his barrel chest, ready for any slicing-and-dicing which might be required if things went kablooey.

"What is the meaning of this sudden intrusion? *WHO DARES TO BARGE IN ON KING RIDLEY KAT?!*" his majesty demanded.

"But we were shown in, Your Maj..." Clover started to say.

"*INSTIGATOR!*" King Ridley yelled.

Clover and Spatchcock panted anxiously, yet stuck their courage to the sticking post and decided to give it a shot.

"Oh great King Ridley Kat..." Clover said.

"*OF YIDDLESMEYER!*" King Ridley bellowed like a true hissyfur.

"Of Yiddlesmeyer," Clover concurred. "We most humbly come to you in our greatest time of need."

"The world of dogs is of no concern to cats. *NOW LEAVE!*" King Ridley meowed, his tail sharply pointing to the nearest exit.

"Cats live in this world too!" Spatchcock spoke up.

"*And many others,*" Tobin chimed in, mysterious as usual as his peeked out from the top of his box.

"I don't take your meaning, ambiguous pup." Ridley snapped back.

"All of Timberton is in grave danger your majesty and time is not on our side." Clover said.

"That natural gas representative, Chinny Finster, is intent on bringing fracking to Timberton." Spatchcock said.

"What's wrong with creating some new jobs?" King Ridley asked. "The economy could certainly use a boost. Nothing wrong with making some money."

"You have to start thinking of long-term effects instead of just short-lived rewards. Fracking is dangerous to the environment." Clover said.

"How? Natural gas is cleaner than coal." King Ridley countered.

"Are you aware of the Greenhouse effect?" Spatch asked.

"That's how they do all those awesome special F/X in Hollywood, right?" King Ridley said, pawing demonstratively at the air.

"No. You're thinking of the green screen effect." Clover answered.

"You dare to tell The King what he's thinks!" Ridley hissed.

"No great king, I just was correcting..."

"You dare correct the king?!"

"Umm...well...okay...let's try...ahh...THIS." Clover suggested.

A loud electro-humming suddenly blared up with an uncanny vibrational intensity. Seconds later, a huge Earth hologram appeared with a blazingly bright atmosphere around it.

"Witchcraft!" King Ridley screamed.

"Actually this is more like the green screen effect." Clover said.

Next a loud sizzling crackling sound blared up quickly followed by a Sun hologram hovering just above the Earth hologram. From its center burning arrows shot forth, penetrating the Earth's atmosphere. Then they bounced back up, but – instead of heading back out into space – they ricocheted off our dirty atmosphere back down to us.

*Illustration by T.L. Stickle*

"You see Your Highness, the Greenhouse effect is when heat from the surface of the earth is absorbed by gases in our atmosphere and then re-radiated everywhere, including back down to Earth." Spatch explained.

"Your point?" King Ridley asked.

"When we burn fossil fuels like coal and natural gas, we intensify the greenhouse effect, causing global warming."

"But natural gas is cleaner than coal, remember?" King Ridley said.

"Yes, but natural gas is basically methane. And when you frack, some of that methane escapes into our atmosphere, which really sucks because it's even better at trapping heat, making it just as bad as coal."

"Thus increasing global warming." King Ridley concluded.

"EXACTLY!" both dogs exclaimed.

"We need clean, carbon-free renewable energy like wind and solar power to be used if we're going to save the environment for us and future generations." Spatchcock said.

"Chinny Finster is a major rep for the fossil fuel industry Your Majesty." Clover said. "And since he's failed to convince the people of Timberton to lease out their land for fracking, he's now planning to burn down ALL of Timberton's rumble-barry trees!"

"Poppycock!" King Ridley cried, popping the giant hologram like a pesky balloon. "Why would anybody do such a stupid destructive thing? You wouldn't be trying to hornswoggle me would you?"

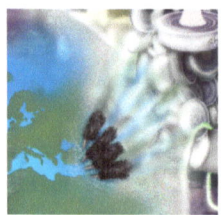

*Illustration by T.L. Stickle*

"Actually Your Highness, these dogs are no fibbers." Abner, a little bespectacled cat smoking a pipe, said.

"Your point?" King Ridley hissed.

"Well I'm a real nosey critter and I can tell you as an eye witness this nefarious twit, Finster, is blinded by his own greed and ambition. He *will* destroy *all* of our rumblebarries."

Illustration by T.L. Stickle

"But why?"

"Because he figures that once our most precious crop has been destroyed for the season, we'll sign over our land – out of economic desperation - rather than starve this winter." Clover said.

"Finster sees the rumblebarries as the last thing standing in his way to buying up Timberton for his fracking plans!" Spatch explained.

"Where are all of the other dogs? Surely they must want to stop this lecherous corporate flunky too?" King Ridley asked.

"Finster dispatched his henchmen dogcatchers to round them up and take them away." Clover said.

"To where?" Ridley asked.

"We don't know." Spatchcock lamented.

"Will you help us thwart our adversaries' rotten plans?" Clover asked.

"Look, I've already taken time out of my busy schedule of playing with boxes, shredding toilet paper, and chasing balls of yarn to listen to you two dogs yip and yap about this so-called predicament."

"So?" Spatch asked.

"Sooooo...YES! *YES I SAY!* YES, THE CATS OF YIDDLESMEYER WILL HELP SAVE TIMBERTON!" Ridley bellowed, so they, every cat in the entire kingdom - and even a few mice over in the next township - could hear his joyous affirmation.

The dogs' tails wagged feverishly.

"Just let me sharpen my claws first." King Ridley grinned.

Chapter 20

# Communication Established

A LOUD CAW bleated from above and Cody looked up just in time to see Ruby releasing the walkie talkie from her talons. The dog traced the radio's drop with eagle eyes, jumping up and catching it in his mouth with razor-sharp precision. He barked a "Thank-You" to the Jackdaw and then quickly read the note.

Mote - hearing his own name crackle from the walkie talkie - unstuck one of his little paws from some putty on a tree so he could answer.

"Cody, this is Mote," the rat said, relieved to have finally established communication. "You need to get to the orchard as quick as possible. Chinny's planning on burning it all down. This is no amateur arsonist work either; he's got some sophisticated incendiary devices filled with high-end accelerants planted all along the perimeter."

"Meaning?" Cody asked.

"I won't be able to diffuse all eight of the frackers' bombs in time. Although Clobber and I have put a major damper on the scummy pyro's plans."

"How many have you disabled so far?" Cody said.

"Five and I'm just getting started with a sixth one. The remaining two are in the south end of the orchard and they're set to detonate at six o'clock."

"Well, it's five thirty right now, can't you just hitch a ride on an arbor drone and zip over to the other two?" Cody asked.

"See that's the problem: the fiendish thugs did some 'under-the-hood improvements,' taking them all out of commission. They even resealed the drones with a blowtorch so as to prevent any easy repairs."

"Creeps thought of everything," Cody barked. "Except for you and Clobber, a couple of good-hearted rascals."

"This is *our* home," Mote said. "Together we will fight to protect it."

"Thank you very much my friend. We're in a tight spot and you've helped tremendously."

"How far away are you all now?"

"We're just about done taking a breather." Cody said. "But I would say maybe four or five miles away yet."

"*Hurry.*" Mote said. "The fire department will be able to help some, but only once the fires have started."

"We'll be there soon, I promise."

*Illustration by T.L. Stickle*

## Chapter 21

# Mad Cat Dash

CLOVER AND SPATCHCOCK had informed King Ridley of the extremely tight timeline they were all forced to work with. As it happened, Ratford Avenue was very far away from the orchard and Ridley immediately knew they would have to procure transportation of some sort. This ride would also have to allow them to approach the target destination with an element of surprise *if* their sneak attack should go off without a hitch.

*Where would they least expect us to show up from?* Ridley wondered.

"Doctor Finicky, I need you to perform a psychic cat scan within a two-mile radius of here." Ridley commanded, smiling as he saw a red moth fluttering up near the ceiling around a light fixture.

"What are you looking for, Your Highness?" the doctor asked.

"Rides. And lots of them."

"As you wish."

Moments later Ridley and his clowder of subjects booked up Ratford Avenue, splitting up into all different directions at the end of the road. Each cat high-tailed it to one of the designated "lifts." These were insipid airheads. With all their prejudiced views, covetous tirades, futile complaining, casual insincerity, and egotistical ramblings, they were mighty powerful sources...*of hot air.* Ridley had quickly devised a plan to make use of them, undertaking a (if somewhat one-sided) community effort.

Once there, they would lasso a strong string – say a fine twine - around the tricky varmint's head. Next – skipping and zipping along from shoulder to shoulder - they would wrap multiple layers of duct tape around the airheads' yapping pie holes, so as to keep all the hot air in. Before you knew it...

*(Mama had a baby and its head popped off!)*
*BOOP!*

The heads popped right off just like bleeding dandelions under flicking thumbs and the cats would hitch a ride into the friendly skies.

Popping June Tecklemeyer's crown off and floating right out the back door, Gus exclaimed, "Now that's how you get ahead in life!"

After their noggins had flown out their windows, the headless bodies would cease flailing their arms about and eventually calm down. A strange relief overcame many of them since now – without mouths – they couldn't be blamed for not using their voices (in a meaningful way). Wondering what to do next, some went to bed and – not needing them anymore – threw their pillows away.

Force of habit, others still stood in front of their bathroom mirrors, brushing at teeth that were no longer there. Minty Atkins – down on Schlerber Avenue - solemnly threw his entire hat collection into a fiery garbage can on his back porch.

Others adapted more easily, and quickly learned how to talk out of their butts, even moreso than usual. Talk about bad breath! Neighbors – who'd managed to keep their heads – overheard the ruckus and thought there was an entire orchestra of sour trumpets.

*Illustration by T.L. Stickle*

*SCHPLART!*

Before long, a fleet of floating tabbies dotted the sky, as they clutched to their huffy-puffy human-head balloons. Some of the lazier cats couldn't even be bothered with clutching, so instead simply tied the strings to their tails and bobbed away amongst the clouds.

*Purr-fect.*

# Chapter 22

# Detonation

THE BIG HAND of the clock clicked into place...
*Six o'clock.*
Mote cringed as he heard the last two bombs detonate in the south end of the orchard, setting it ablaze. They were more like scorching blasts than loud bangs. The fire quickly began to engulf the rumblebarry trees, but Mote and Clobber were helpless but to watch. All they could do was wait for the dogs' arrival.

His ears perked up once again as he heard another muted explosion somewhere in the distance, quickly followed by what sounded like a crunching crash. There was no way those noises were coming from within the orchard.

Maybe from across town?
But where though?
And why?
*Hurry Cody, just as fast as you can.* Mote thought with increasing panic.
**BOOM!**
A deafening explosion blasted, chased by a massive splintering crash. Old Oren, an eighty-five year-old oak tree – one of Timberton's honorary citizens - fell in front of the fire

house. Twigs, branches, and limbs were torn from his trunk in a cacophony of snapping, thrashing, and cracking. Leaves shot out everywhere in a dervish of disorientation. The majestic tree had been over fifty feet tall and four feet thick and had been climbed, nested in, picnicked under, and beloved by many.

Now poor Old Oren lay dying, the base of his trunk smoldering ruins, blasted into smithereens. Old Effie, a seventy-seven year-old water tower, screamed as she watched her steady friend die across town, a hole in the horizon where he once stood. As tears slid down her steely cheeks, she fondly remembered her fellow giant.

Nothing lasts forever.

And some things are gone too soon.

The firefighters on duty had their shock amplified when they heard the fire alarm right after the enormous explosion and crash, quickly realizing the huge oak tree now completely blocked the two large garage doors. Knowing people needed help, but unable to respond made them feel at a loss. There was nowhere to go now.

"Seems to be coming from the orchard." Firefighter Rick said.

"It'll take us hours just to clear this mess out of the way so we can get the fire engines back on the road." Firefighter Martina said.

Fire Chief Flankston sighed, not liking any of this, not one bit.

"Contact Ironton," he said. "They're the nearest township."

"But they're over seventy miles away!" Firefighter Rick exclaimed.

"I know, but other than pray for rain, there's nothing else we can do. Not to mention, we've helped them in the past, so they'll be more than happy to lend a hand." Chief Flankston replied. "Now everybody find as many axes and chainsaws as you can and let's at least begin to get to work on this massive tree which has us blocked in."

"*Oren,*" Firefighter Martina said as a frown sunk in.

From a lone blue car parked nearby in a vacant lot, Melvin smiled.

"Perfect landing," he spoke into his walkie-talkie. "The fire department has officially been taken out of the picture. Those trucks aren't going anywhere."

"Excellent." Chinny responded. "Get over to the orchard to make sure things are going as planned."

"Roger that." Melvin said as he drove away.

Chapter 23

# It's Lovely Up Here

KING RIDLEY OF Yiddlesmeyer and his entire squadron of cats floated amongst the dreamy clouds. A steady breeze sailed them closer to their target, the rumblebarry orchard.

Only about fifteen minutes into their flight, Ridley saw a large black bird approaching them from the south. All this unforeseen aviation had worked up an appetite in the formidable tabby and his tummy growled. For just a moment Ridley imagined the bird roasted to perfection, and decked out with all the trimmings…even those cute little frills on her juicy tender legs. He licked his chops as the winged prey approached. However, the bird kept its distance, but lightly flapped its wings so as to keep hovering within hearing range.

"I'm Ruby," the beautiful onyx Jackdaw cawed. "and I mean you no harm and hope you mean me none as well. May I ask what all you cats are doing up here?"

"Not that it's any of your business," Ridley said. "But we're en route to the rumblebarry orchard to help stop it from burning down."

"Same here, and thanks for helping out." Ruby cawed back.

"All creatures, great and small, have a stake in today's outcome." Ridley stated.

"Very true." Ruby said, eyeing the airheads with their blathering mouths taped up nice and shut. "It's very peaceful up here today."

"Tell me about it. I almost feel like snuggling up in one of those cozy clouds for a cat nap, but duty prevails." Ridley answered.

"Amazing what you can do with a little hot air."

"You mean a *lot* of hot air." Ridley laughed. "Have you seen all the dogs by any chance?"

"As a matter of fact, I just delivered a walkie-talkie to them. They're a few miles ahead of us, but are headed in the same direction."

"Excellent. For those would-be destroyers, it'll be raining cats and dogs today." Ridley said.

"Well, raining *cats* at least." Ruby laughed. "I'll see you there."

"Soon, comrade, very soon." Ridley said as he watched the bird fly off ahead of them.

# Chapter 24

# Orchard on Fire

THE FIRE WAS gaining power as it devoured the first row of rumblebarry trees, incinerating the tender bark with fiery bites and scorching swallows. Sizzling and popping, the barries splattered dark hot jelly over the autumnal foliage. If the blaze managed to burn its way through the next row, then it would surely grow into an all-out conflagration and destroy most of the orchard.

Cody and the pack burst out of the underbrush, having smelled the smoke from miles away. Panting for breath, all the dogs dropped to the ground for a moment's rest.

"I don't think we're gonna be able to rely on the fire department for any help," Clammy said.

"Why's that?" Cody said.

"I just have a hunch, something doesn't feel right."

The chocolate lab grimaced and then marched right up to a tree where Mote – still astride Clobber – was just finishing defusing another bomb.

"Nice work my friend." Cody remarked, tugging some burrs off his coat.

Mote bit through a red wire and then pointed over his shoulder. "If it's any consolation, the last two bombs are near-ish the water tower."

"Ohhh..." Cody considered.

Almost fifty yards from the fire stood Effie, the orchard's own little water tower. The rusty old ironbelly had certainly seen better days, but still possessed a handsome, weathered appearance. The bottom was shaped like the head of a silver bullet while on top warped shingles formed a funnel roof. Creeping crimson kudzu dripped from the railings and festooned itself across the sides.

Emblazoned on the tank's iron hide were large faded black letters:

**TIMBERTON**

"Yes, I figured just maybe it could come in handy, but it won't be easy." Mote explained.

"Why's that?"

"Remember that huge thunderstorm, the one that cut off everyone's power for a couple of hours?"

"Yes, how could I forget? The thunder boomed so loud, windows were shaking." Cody remembered. "First rumbling, and then clashing louder and louder."

"The lightning was fierce and fantastic all night too." Mote said. "One bolt struck the water tower's ladder, destroying most of it."

"That was just a couple weeks ago. Nobody has gotten around to fixing it yet."

"Thanks to the arbor drones, nobody ever really had to get up there, so I guess it wasn't exactly a priority." Mote noted.

*"Until now."* Cody moaned.

"I'm afraid so. When automation fails, we have to resort to manual operation. Which – without a ladder – I don't even think is possible."

The dog and rat slowly raised their heads. Way up – a good twenty feet above them – was the tank's drainage valve, its iron handwheel glaring in the hot sun. The damaged ladder's lowest rung was still at least seventeen feet above them, blackened and ravaged from where it was hit.

Cody scanned the distance from the ground up to the handwheel.

*So close and yet so far away.*

Attempting to climb it would end in disaster. One of the tower's front legs had been struck by the lightning as well, leaving its structural integrity severely compromised. Even with a gentle breeze, the iron giant slightly buckled, a strained whine creaking from its old bones.

"It's completely out of reach," Maisey said. "I don't think there's much we can do here."

Cody ran past the two rows of burning trees, to get a better view of the fire's progress.

*CRACK!*

Cody looked up and rolled quickly out of the way of a fiery branch which crashed to the ground, almost burning his tail. He could see there was an irrigation route of perhaps thirty feet between this row and the main orchard.

Time was precious and the chocolate lab had to think fast. He was a leader and he was a water dog, and in a jam like this, you could do a lot worse.

He called over Dagmar.

She booked over to him in seconds flat. "Yesch Kody? Vat's up?"

"Dagmar," Cody said. "I need you to round up all the dogs with the biggest, bushiest tails as quick as you possibly can."

"Vy?" Dagmar asked.

"I'll explain later, just get it done." Cody replied.

"Vill do." Dagmar said, running off.

"By the way, how's your memory these days Daggy?"

"Scharp as efer, vy?"

"You'll see." Cody answered.

Next Cody called over Turk.

"Turk, I need to you to grab the beefiest mutts you know and go fetch those arbor drones, all four of them." Cody barked.

"But Cody, they're broken-sabotaged-*KAPUT*, all of them!" Turk cried.

"It doesn't matter, I think I have a good idea of how we can repurpose them." Cody said. "Now I know you can't fly them, so just roll them like giant steel coins."

"Where to?" Turk asked.

"Right in front of the water tower." Cody said.

"I'm on it." Turk said, charging off to get the big dogs.

Cody now ran back to the front of the fire, dodging fiery debris along the way. He looked up at the water tower looming over them.

"It's *waaaaaaaay* out of reach." Spatchcock winced at the sheer height.

"So it would seem." Cody said.

"Well, the ladder's gone," Fibbledip said. "Which makes it pretty much inaccessible to us."

"This is a challenge I don't think any of us are up to Cody." Mister Sparky said.

"We ARE up to it my friends." Cody insisted. "And in the face of such a deadly challenge, we only have one option left."

All the dogs looked at Cody in wide-eyed anticipation.

"WE MUST STAND TALL." Cody said. "AND WE MUST DO IT TOGETHER."

"How?" Cooper asked. "Our fur can easily catch fire too!"

"Hold that thought," Cody said, seeing Dagmar headed straight towards him with a pack of the bushiest tailed dogs amongst them.

"Okay Kody, now vat?" Dagmar asked.

"Follow me."

Cody quickly led the dogs to the service way. He had them make a tight line across it, so that their tails were facing the fiery row of burning trees.

"My furry-tailed friends, YOU all are here to buy us a little time." Cody barked. "If that fire gets past this service way it will reach the main orchard and at that point – I'm afraid – all will be lost."

The dogs whined and some pouted.
"But this is no time to have your tails between your legs," Cody instructed. "Just the opposite in fact."

Some of the dogs' ears perked up at this.

"Remember that time Skip got his head stuck in a peanut butter jar?" Cody asked.

The dogs immediately laughed and began wagging their tails.

"Yes, *YES!*" Cody barked. "That's all you have to do: BE HAPPY! THINK HAPPY THOUGHTS!"

"Why?" asked Bear, a Keeshond.

"Because we need your tails wagging faster than they ever have!" Cody barked. "All together, your tail wagging will help blow the fire *away* from the rest of the orchard, at least for a little while."

"That's not going to be easy," Maisey moaned.

"That's true, that's why Dagmar here is going to help out by taking you all on a trip down memory lane, only happy thoughts of course." Cody replied.

Dagmar nodded, "Comen on gang, ven you sink about it, vee are pretty vakky kreachers." The dogs nodded right back, their tails already beginning to rev up for the job.

"Dagmar, when you hear me howl I need you and all these dogs to run right back up here to the front. And don't drag your paws either; otherwise you'll all be riding the rumblebarry rapids." Cody directed.

"I'll be waitink vor your schignal sen." She said.

"Thank you friends, and thank you Daggy." Cody said, now returning to the water tower where Turk and his crew were just rolling in the four arbor drones.

"Excellent." Cody said. "Now I need you to position them just right."

"How so?" Clover asked.

"That's something I'm not sure of just yet." Cody said. "It will all depend."

"On what?" Clover said.

"Gravity." Cody answered.

"GRAVY?" Smokey said, licking his chops.

"No, *gravity*." Cody replied, and then fell silent as he looked up at the tower again.

"What's he doing?" Smokey asked. "Does he see a bird up there?"

"No silly, he's sizing it up." Clover answered.

"Okay, here's what we're going to do." Cody barked. "We're going to turn on the water tower's drainage valve."

"*HOW?!?*" many of the dogs barked, bewildered.

"We're going to rise to the challenge, literally." Cody said. "Mop and Turk, I want you to stand in front of the water tower. The Komondor and Newfoundland stood side by side, each almost three feet tall. Clearly these big strong dogs would make an excellent foundation, but Cody thought twice. He saw the hundreds of thick cords making up Mop's scatter-brained fur and saw great potential. (And not to clean up some sloppy spill on the kitchen floor either.) Then he noticed Turk's tail, which resembled a large feather duster.

"Actually, I want you two to go back and help Dagmar and the other dogs with fire-control." Cody barked. "Mop, tell Daggy I gave *you* special orders, to do something a little different from the rest of the dogs."

"What's that?" Mop said, blowing some cords out of his eyes.

"Chase your own tail, and chase it *fast*."

"Fast?"

"Like you're a tornado, spinning out of control."

"Will I spin out of control?"

"With Dagmar supervising? Hardly."

"Does it matter if I barf after a while?"

"Not at all. Just don't lick it up."

Both dogs laughed.

"Okay, you two head back there."

The dogs made tracks.

## Chapter 25

# Fur Ladder To The Sky

OKAY Dozer, I need you, Marsha, and Slabfork to stand in front of the water tower instead." The Mastiff shook some drool off his formidable jowls and then took his place alongside the Pit Bull and the St. Bernard.

"Now you three are going to be our new foundation, so I need you all to huddle close together." The dogs did, but Cody still noticed some slight gaps between them. "Squeeze even tighter together, like you're sardines." They did, so much so their muscles were beginning to writhe under the pressure. Slabfork, caught in the middle, groaned as the pitty and massy shoved into him from opposite sides.

"Brace yourselves, my friends." Cody said, jumping onto their backs, so that his front paws rested on Marsha's back, while his hind legs balanced on Dozer's. Along with Slabfork, the three beefy dogs made a heck of a foundation to help anchor them.

"Somebody needs to cut down on the rumblebarry pie." Marsha quipped.

"HA!" Cody barked. "Okay Buford, you hop up here next to me." Cody said.

Buford clumsily mounted the taller dogs' backs, taking his place next to Cody.

"Okay, next I need two medium-sized dogs to hop on our backs." Cody barked.

"You're building a ladder!" Mister Sparky cried.

"Not just any ladder, Sparks. A *fur* ladder." Cody answered. "When we all stand together we can reach the top. Nanner, I want you to remain on the ground at all times to be my eyes." Cody said.

The yellow Afghan hound looked up confused, "Your eyes?"

"Yes, you have extremely keen vision and I need you to use your eyes to help chart our progress."

"Gotcha! Twenty-twenty baby. *Cha-cha-cha!*" Nanner exclaimed, his curly tail swaying back and forth.

\* \* \* \* \* \* \* \* \* \* \* \* \* \* \* \* \* \* \* \* \* \* \* \* \* \* \* \* \* \* \* \*

Dagmar struggled for clarity as her eyes constantly shifted between the double spectacle of the Komondornado and the looming Wall of Fire just beyond him. As Mop chased his tail each ropey cord of fur stood out on end, slicing through the air one whoosh after the next. To his credit (and Cody's), he was generating a *lot* of wind power, helping to hold the relentless fire in place...yet sort of stoking it simultaneously.

Dagmar was lulled into a daze as she stared at the dancing flames which were shimmering in waves of heat distortion like a seductive mirage. The inferno held a strange power over the elegant beast, the very air around her rippling hypnotically.

Ssssssssss...the hiss of sizzling sap rose up around her like a sea of static. Her ears pressed down on her formidable skull while her front paws lightly scraped the ground, leaving tiny trenches in the earth.

Dagmar's large glassy eyes grew heavy for a moment, until a large branch – burned straight through – snapped off a trunk hitting the ground with a loud crash. Ripped out of her trance, she continued to urgently spew memories at the tail-wagging dogs.

"Sink of ven you see your human for see firscht time after he or she hasch just returned from a long vakation. Sink of how much you mist sem! Sink of jumpink into seir arms again ant schmooching sem all ofer!" Dagmar reminisced. Maisey, Kelly, Samson, and the other dogs were growing increasingly weary, but they were keeping the flames at bay, for the time being.

Anytime Dagmar would see a flame trying to span the gap, she would beef up the Good Energy by relying on one word – so tried and true – that all dogs were helplessly susceptible to:

"VAHK!" Dagmar barked. "Voo vants to go for das VAHK?"

The dogs' tails wagged fast and furious, and the flames were pushed back once more.

But how much longer could they keep this up?

Chapter 26

# Human Scratching Posts

MEANWHILE, FESTERING ON the other end of the orchard, Melvin, Gretchen, and Bilge were checking out the other (now defused) bombs, trying to figure out why they had failed to detonate, but mostly just blaming each other.

"You're an incompetent boob." Gretchen yelled at Bilge. "You didn't even properly arm these bombs!"

"Like heck Gretch!" Bilge barked back. "They were all properly armed. Why would the two over by the water tower go off and none of the rest?"

Melvin picked up the bomb and slid it under his fat, slobbering nose, sniffing at it like a fresh bouquet of cold cuts. His greasy schnozzola left smears of snot on it like a particularly repugnant trail of snail slime.

"I smell a rat." Melvin said. "Maybe even a cat too."

"What are you saying?" Gretchen asked.

"I'm saying somebody has sabotaged our sabotage. Double-crossed us."

"We made sure there weren't any people around when we prepped." Bilge said.

Melvin looked up into the branches of the trees, squinting his beady little eyes, trying to hone in on any unnatural movement.

"I don't think *people* are our problem." Melvin said. "I think this orchard and these trees happen to have friends, of all shapes and sizes."

"Gremlins?" Bilge asked, breaking wind.

Gretchen sighed and rolled her eyes, "No Dingleberry Jones, not gremlins. Not gnomes. Or even mutant pigeons."

"Other animals..." Bilge mumbled, almost under his breath.

"Yes, other animals, just like those pesky dogs no doubt." Melvin said.

"*Other animals...*" Bilge repeated, this time louder.

"We heard you the first time." Gretchen said. "Now we have to reactivate these bombs and fast, or Chinny's..."

"*OTHER ANIMALS!*" Bilge shouted this time, pointing up to the sky.

"AMBUSH FROM ABOVE!" Melvin screamed.

Dozens of cats dropped out of the sky, the entire furry armada relinquishing their airhead balloons, which floated higher and higher, each making a nice, juicy POPPY implosion upon reaching the upper regions of our polluted atmosphere.

*Popskulls!*

"*IT'S MAIMING TIME!*" King Ridley roared.

The spazz-kitties plopped onto Gretchen, Bilge, and Melvin and began their attack. Desperate to score a hiding place, Melvin tried crawling through the leaves but was suddenly lifted way up into the air as Indomitus Minx bit down on his legs and began to feed on the fiend, who had a taffy-like chewiness.

"Mmm...*GOOT-GOOT!*" the hybrid dino-kitty groaned between chomps.

Two groups of cats lassoed Gretchen's wrists and pulled her between two hammock trees.

"Hey Vince," Tabbalena called over to the group on the opposite side.

"What it be Tabbypoo," Vince replied.

"Let's play tug-o-war!"

"Now you're talking!"

They split old Gretch like a banana, right down the middle as Bilge's screams bellowed in the background. Her greasy gopher guts splattered to the ground with an obscene plop.

\* \* \* \* \* \* \*

The carnage was a gruesome sight to behold. Yet the gory aftermath had a glimmering crimson allure the bloodthirsty cats found irresistible, like the burning ruby sun of their home planet Schlar.

"Well gang, looks like man flesh is back on the menu!" King Ridley of Yiddlesmeyer declared.

A furry feeding frenzy ensued as the cats dove into the pile of bloody remains and feasted like a school of purranha.

Clearly, no meat wagons would be needed today...

*...but a hose would've helped.*

*"I'VE GOT BLISTERS ON MY WHISKERS!"* Abner exclaimed half crazed.

Near the end of their picnic, BBK aka *BooBoo Kitty*, a little tiny mix of a cat, had a whole leg (Bilge's right to be precise) to himself. Boo pouted for a moment, wondering if his eyes just might be bigger than his tummy.

*It's too much meat.*

BBK suddenly stood up on his hind legs – more hangry than ever before - and hollered like a grizzly alligator.

*Naaaah, I got this.*

Then, much to the rest of the cats' stunned senses, BBK's mouth stretched open. *Really wide.*

He unhinged his jaw and lowered it like a draw bridge for maximum carnivorous efficiency, the ligament stretching apart like a rubber band, sort of like when a snake sucks down a moose. Next, a slimy purple forked tongue lashed out of BBK's heaving, pulsing fanged pie hole and lassoed itself around the torn off limb. Slowly it dragged Bilge's meaty leg across the grass and into the dark cavernous tunnel of his little pussycat throat.

A flock of vultures circled above, witnessing the insatiable cats eat up practically everything in sight.

"*Oh dear*, hopefully the furry little trashgoblins will save *something* for us," fretted Craven the Vulture.

BBK made a most unpleasant schlupping sound as he sucked the meaty man leg down his hatch. Within two minutes little old Boo had swallowed the entire leg, his fury body now completely engorged like a swollen clubfoot.

"Dang BBK, you sure got a lot of appetite for such a tiny tabby!" Grim said.

BBK only smiled, belched loudly, and then giggled. All the other cats laughed too as they licked gore off their little paws.

"Come now, my noble – *and apparently insatiable* - subjects," King Ridley beckoned. "We have diligently performed our duty and now will return back to our kingdom to celebrate."

All the cats meowed their approval.

"Are we gonna partake of some catnip?" Vince asked.

"Of course." King Ridley said.

"Are we gonna get all squeezy and cozy in our favorite boxes?" Gus asked.

"As snug as a bug in a rug." King Ridley answered.

"Are we gonna indulge in some stinky sardine pudding?" Seline inquired, licking her chops.

"It wouldn't be a celebration without it!" King Ridley exclaimed, licking a dewdrop of blood hanging from the end of one of his whiskers.

"Are we going to sharpen our claws by shredding your antique wall tapestries to tattered threads and fibers? Huh? *HUH?*" Plik asked, rather excited.

"Now you're just pushing your luck." King Ridley said on a sober note. "Besides, I have a whole stack of pro-fracking coloring books you can shred instead."

"Now *there's* some cheap propaganda really worth shredding!" Plik exclaimed as his claws sprung out and he made a tearing motion through the air. And with that, the cats left the orchard and danced the *CHA-CHA-CHA* all the way home.

Unbeknownst to the departing felines, Chinny was up in a nearby tree, hiding out until the slaughter ended. Only when the very last cat's tail was almost out of sight, did he finally come down. He saw one of his henchmen's skulls and walked over to it.

"Idiots." he said, crushing it under his boot.

*CRUNCH!*

"If this is going to be done right, then clearly I'm going to have to do it myself."

## Chapter 27

# Race To The Top

"SORRY MATE," FRANK said to Slabfork as he stepped on his snout, taking his first step on the dog ladder. "Pardon me." he then said to Buford as his paw slipped off his ear.

"Ouch!" Gage exclaimed as Frank's claws sunk a little too deep into his back.

"My bad." Frank said, trying his best to get his footing down.

"It's okay, just be careful." Gage replied, focusing on the beam in front of him. Cody had instructed all the dogs, once they were in position, to focus on just one spot. This helped increase their sense of balance and the overall stability of the often-tottering canine tower.

Sally lurched up next, taking her place next to Frank. Her legs were wobbly as she looked down.

"Whoa." She said. "I'm getting kind of queasy. Never been this high off the ground before."

"Don't look down." Frank said. "In fact, just pick a spot on the water tower and focus on it, that way you'll become less dizzy."

"Thank you Frank."

"Anytime Sally."

For better or for worse – decidedly worse – Clammy lucked out and had Smokey on top of him, continuously shifting his paws all up and down his spine, nonstop like a demented chiropractor.

"Be still Smokey, be still." Clammy said, becoming increasingly peeved.

"I am still. Why don't *you* try to be still?" Smokey barked back again.

Ever since hopping on top of him, the hyper wiener dog had been nagging the Dalmatian constantly.

"Stop wobbling. Stop wobbling so much!"

"If I was any more still I'd be a statue." Clammy growled.

"Be still already!" Smokey barked, once again shifting his paws about. "Be still!"

"Oh, get off my back!" Clammy barked, finally fed up enough.

The kooky dachshund – not the shiniest apple on the tree – actually then lifted three of his paws as if to comply with the foul-tempered firedog, sending a massive tremor up and down the entire dog ladder.

"No you silly mutt! Not literally!" Clammy barked.

Clover quickly grabbed Smokey by the ear so as to stop him from tumbling down the fur ladder.

The sudden shift in weight caused a chain reaction of instability which was throwing Doggie Mountain off balance.

"WHOA!" all the dogs said as the entire fur ladder began to sway and totter, getting precariously close to tipping over altogether.

"Just hang on runt and this'll be over before you blow it," Clammy told Smokey as the freaked dachshund grabbed hold of his spotted tail.

"What the heck is going on up there?" Cody barked from below.

"Sorry." Smokey yipped.

Roxie chomped down on Buford's tail for a little more balance. The other dogs had had their fill of tail-biting from the cave though and decided to throw caution to the wind and remain untethered.

Cody growled. "Nanner, about how much farther do we have to go before we reach the valve?"

The Afghan hound tilted his head upwards over the bodies of the dogs, trying to measure from the top of the latest rung of dogs to the water tower's handwheel.

"Well Cody, I'd have to estimate you still have a gap of about seven feet left until you reach the drainage valve." Nanner replied.

"Okay, it's going to be awfully close everybody." Cody said. "Now listen up small, but stout-hearted dogs still on the ground: I need you to now go up separately, as I call you. And when you reach the top, you will NOT be huddling in twos or threes anymore. Instead, you will be standing on each others' backs, one-by-one, so as to reach the maximum height. Understood?"

The last few dogs, looked uneasy, yet barked their affirmations all the same.

"Excellent. Okay, Mister Sparky, you're going up first."

The pug closed his eyes, took a deep breath and began to scale Doggie Mountain as if it were Everest.

"Fibbledip, you're next. And no yodeling allowed!"

The Boston terrier smiled, mounted the ladder, and showed some real grit and as he hustled his little self all the way to the top.

"Okay Nanner, what now?" Cody said.

"Maybe three feet, give or take an inch or two."

Spatchcock was the only small dog left on the ground. His head slowly wavered in sync with the dog-ladder. His tummy tingled.

"I think I have vertigo." Spatchcock said.

"Don't look down, even when you're only halfway up." Sally called down to Spatchcock. "Or you just might blow chunks on Cody."

The chocolate lab looked up and growled. The Rhodesian ridgeback chuckled a dry chuckle.

Cody called on Spatchcock.

Spatch hesitated, shivering as a fresh wave of icy panic froze him to the ground.

*I can't do this.*

*They picked the wrong dog for this job.*

*I'm afraid of heights.*

*I'll fall.*

*I'll fail.*

*I'm failing right now in fact.*

The tiny Chihuahua's thoughts turned against him as panic began to overtake him.

The goblin smirked at him as it ran its thorny claws over his tiny head.

Marsha, Slabfork, and Dozer were beginning to crack under the pressure. Together their dozen legs were trembling as they forced them to remain locked in an upright position. They felt they could all collapse under the strenuous weight at any moment.

Clover saw Spatchcock down on the ground, looking too afraid to even hop on.

**And she knew.**

# Chapter 28

# The Boost

"HURRY! *HURRY!* WE don't know how much longer we can hold on!" Marsha barked, straining to even speak now. But Spatchcock was frozen to the spot and didn't look like he was going anywhere anytime soon.

And then something wonderful happened.

"I know what you're doing my friend." Clover said, from high up on the fur ladder.

"You do?" Spatchcock answered.

"You're listening to the wrong voice aren't you? You're letting the goblin drive again."

Flushed with embarrassment, Spatch could barely speak, but he did.

"I might be."

"Well kick him out of your car, *NOW*, because there's another voice deep inside you, isn't there?"

"Maybe."

"And what is the other voice saying to you right now?"

"He's saying, he says...that maybe, just maybe...I can do this."

"And do YOU think you can do this?" Clover asked her friend.

"I think I can do this." Spatchcock said.

"*Know* you can do this. Know it with every single ounce of who you are my sweet friend."

His heart racing like mad, he opened the driver door, and used his entire body to shove the Goblin out from behind his steering wheel. Gobby was flung at a fire hydrant head-first...*THWUMP!*...as the little dog sped away, leaving him in the dust.

*Then he took control.*

Spatch lifted one paw off the ground and placed it on Dozer's side.

"Know you can, little buddy." Dozer said, nodding him on.

For him getting atop Dozer was like mounting a Brontosaurus, and he slipped off, pouting a little.

"No biggie. Lemme get you started," Dozer said, gently lifting Spatch by the nape of his neck onto Slabfork's head. From there he saw the large Bloodhound above him.

"Buford, would you mind if I used your ear to help pull myself up?"

"You do what you gotta do little buddy." Buford replied.

Up another double-dog rung, Spatch exhaled.

"You're doing great, just keep going." Cody said.

Placing his paws on the chocolate lab's snout, Spatch used one of Gage's jutting hocks as a step up onto Roxie's butt.

"Sorry," Spatch said.

"Thuurrt's okaaay." Rox replied through a mouthful of Buford's tail.

"Over here."

Spatch took a slight step up onto Gage's back where he saw Frank slowly moving his left hind foot back and forth.

"Grab hold mate," Frank said.

Spatch did just that and the Catahoula Leopard Hound gently lifted his leg up as high as he could.

"Careful...careful." Sally whispered.

"Thanks Frank," Spatch said, as he now could move across moreso instead of up. He walked under Clammy's spotted leg and used Kelly's fur to help hoist himself up to Smokey *and* Clover. He quickly snuggled his little snout behind her ear.

"I love you my friend." he said.

"I love you too, and I love that you're listening to *your* voice and not his." she said.

"Ditto backatcha!"

Spatch climbed on her back and then over Mister Sparky's head and right up onto Fibbledip's back.

"About time you got here." Fibbledip said.

The little Chihuahua only glared at him.

"Just kidding!"

Spatch look up over to the handwheel which was not only a good couple feet across from him, but also looked incredibly smooth, dare he say 'slippery?' A light breeze came on and he clenched his paws into Fibbledip's back, to help keep him from swaying.

"We got a problem here." Spatchcock said, almost ashamed to admit it, after all this trouble.

"What?" Fibbledip asked.

Then, much louder this time, "The handwheel's too slippery; I'll fall if I try to grab hold of it!"

Many of the dogs groaned upon hearing this.

"Row rut?" Roxie said.

"Whatever it is, you all better hurry up." Dozer yelled.

"We can't hold on much longer." Marsha barked.

The foundation dogs' legs were now buckling under the tremendous weight of all the ascending rungs of canines above them.

"You strong?" Slabfork barked.

"I'm strong!" Marsha barked back.

"You solid?" Slabfork barked.

"We're solid!" Dozer and Marsha barked back.

"We gonna break down and collapse any moment now?" Slabfork barked.

"*Most definitely,*" all three answered in unison.

*Illustration by T.L. Stickle*

Flying towards the orchard Ruby shook her beak, gobsmacked, upon beholding the towering fur ladder, a true feat of canine collaboration if there ever was one. She flew through a cloud, vaguely wondering if she was really tasty cotton candy in her beak.

"Cody, may *I* help?" a small, but familiar voice called out.

"Who or what is that?" Cody asked, hearing a warped and very sour attempt at some misbegotten theme music.

That furry little saddle tramp Mote appeared atop Clobber, wheezing into a tiny silver harmonica.

"Mote!" Cody barked, glad to see him. "Besides promising never to play that thing ever again, how can you help?"

Mote threw Cody a sarcastic smile, tucked his mousey harmonica into Clobber's saddle bag and withdrew a large blue bandana. "This just might do the trick."

"Go for it." Cody said. And with that Clobber sprang onto the dog ladder and started climbing.

"Watch the claws pal." Sally barked.

"You'll heal." Mote hissed, not having any time for petty grievances.

Once they'd reached Clover and Smokey, Mote and Clobber paused to call up to the rest of the single-rung dogs.

"Mr. Sparky, Fibbledip, and Spatchcock, I need you all to listen to me for a moment." Mote called up to them.

They carefully looked down at the little white rat atop his mangy cat steed, wondering why he was even up here with them.

"At the count of seven, Clobber and I are going to shoot up the rest of this ladder and unto the railing right next to the handwheel. So right now, I need you all to seriously brace yourselves. Okay?"

All the dogs dug their paws into each others' backs and once they all felt fortified, they barked their readiness.

"One..." Mote said, tightening his grasp on Clobber's reins.

"Two..." jingling his spurs.

"Three!" kicking them hard into the cat-steed's sides. Clobber meowed loudly and raced up the remaining fur ladder like a Fourth of July rocket. He then sprang his two kitty paws right off the top of Spatch's head, bouncing himself right onto the railing next to the handwheel. Mote quickly tied one end of the bandana to one of the handwheel's upper spokes.

"What happened to four-five-six and seven?" Spatch asked.

Mote giggled nervously a bit, "It's not like we have all day."

The end of the bandana looked much more secure to Spatchcock.

"Okay Spatch, here's what we're gonna do." Mote said. "I want you to jump up and grab the end of the bandana with your mouth. Once you have it, you're going to hang onto it with your dear life, using the weight of your entire body to help turn the valve."

"I guess you mean what I'M going to do." Spatch replied.

"We're all in this together my friend." Mote said. "You need a countdown?"

"Only if I get ALL of it this time." Spatch quipped.

Mote giggled. "Just go for it then."

He almost did, but then he didn't. Spatchcock's ears perked up as he heard a ghostly gurgling – strange indigestion – come rumbling from deep within Effie's ironbelly.

...*yyyaaaaaaggggaaaaahhhhhhnnnaaaaafaaaaaahhhhh...*

Spatchcock's ears pressed down as fearful recognition struck.

"What's wrong?" Mote asked.

Spatchcock didn't hear him, but he did hear...

*Don't do it! You will die! Don't do it! You will die! Don't do it!*

He shook his head and looked over at the blue bandana and blinked a few times.

*Could it really be?*

Why, it was his bag of treats...just waiting for him.

"Spatch, where's your head at?" Fibbledip said.

...*yooooooorrrrrggggguuunnnnaaafaaaaaaaahhhhl....*

*SHUT UP!*

Silence. Sweet silence.

Not needing another nudge, the little Chihuahua lunged down on his haunches and sprang up into the air, leaping across and catching the bandana in his mouth.

A loud metallic groan creaked, then silence. Just not as sweet this time.

"What's happening up there?" Cody asked Nanner.

"They've got a banana, I mean a bandana tied to the handwheel and Spatchcock's hanging off it. It looks like they're trying to use his weight to turn the valve on, but there's just one problem." Nanner responded.

"WHAT?"

"Spatch is a Chihuahua, which means he barely weighs anything. And that's not going to be enough to turn that handwheel."

*Illustration by T.L. Stickle*

Nanner was right too, Spatch was just kind of hanging there like an adorable wind sock, smiling from ear to ear.

"Annee..ting...happa...neen?" Spatch asked Mote, through his clenched teeth.

"Not just yet, but I have another idea." Mote replied. He looked down at the other dogs, as if calculating something. "It's probably going to take a few of these pipsqueaks."

"Whaaa?" Spatch tried to ask.

"Okay Fibbs, you're up next. We need more weight, so you need to jump up next and hold onto Spatch's tail with *your* dear life. I can count..." Mote didn't even have time to finish as the Boston terrier hopped off Mister Sparky's head and latched onto Spatch's tail.

"Ouch!" Spatch grumbled.

"Sorry." Fibbledip tired to apologize through a mouthful of dog tail.

This time the entire water tower shuddered followed by a soft crunching sound. Unfortunately the handwheel still didn't budge.

"Okay Mister Sparky, you're up next." Mote called down.

Another light crunching sound, but that was it.

"Smokey, please hop up and grab Sparky's tail." Mote said.

As the fur ladder converted into a fur chain, Mote's ears perked up as he now heard a distinct rusty creaking coming from the handwheel.

"We're getting there my friends!" Mote exclaimed. "Clover, grab a mouthful of Smokey's tail."

After the beagle grabbed the dachshund's tail, the handwheel visibly began to turn - the weight of the crew now too great to resist anymore. Mote's beady red eyes bulged out of their sockets as the iron handwheel slowly, ever so slowly, began to make a downward clockwise motion. At first fat drops and then small rivulets of water came from the drainage valve, but the full release was still being held back.

Cody, seeing the collecting pool of water under the tower, howled his signal. He knew they must be getting awfully close. Dagmar, Mop, Turk, and the other dogs quickly returned to the water tower, although their worn-out tails hung limp from exhaustion.

"Okay, all you big dogs need to prop up these arbor drones right under the water tower, which is going to burst any second now." Cody barked, shaking under the strain of the other dogs' weight too.

As it turned out, they would have more than a second or two.

"NO!" Mote yelled as he noticed the handwheel had stopped moving again. There was that crackling crunching sound again. Then nothing.

The water tower clearly wasn't cooperating with the dogs that day and instead, was demanding one more good tug before giving up its reservoir.

"We'll see about that." Clammy barked, as he sprung off of Frank's back. He took a bite of Clover's tail and didn't let go.

BOOM!

The Dalmatian was the final link needed to yank the chain. As the handwheel finally finished its rotation, the drainage valve released a huge current of water. It fell down onto the flat surfaces of the arbor drones the dogs were beginning to pry up.

The water splashed violently about as it ricocheted in multiple directions. One powerful surge struck what was left of the dog tower, washing them away as an avalanche of fur came tumbling down. The medium-sized dogs sort of pancaked onto the larger ones, but the chain was still barely hanging on.

Spatch's teeth were on the verge of being pulled out and his neck muscles felt like they were being torn apart. Clammy was confident in his own physical agility and let go of Clover's tail. Dropping, he quickly stepped down the stack of furry pancakes back to earth.

"IIIIIccccaaaannnttthhhhoollld-ddonnnnaaannnnnnnymmooorrre!!" Spatch screeched through bleeding gums.

The dogs all looked up just as the chain fell off the water tower. Clammy spun around and caught Smokey on his back. Cody leapt over Turk to catch Clover before she could hit the ground. Slabfork made a soft landing for Mister Sparky. Roxie

sat her butt down so Fibbledip could use her back to slide safely down the stack. Timing it perfectly, Nanner sprung off Marsha's back into the air to catch Spatch by his tail before he could crash.

The little Chihuahua spit out some blood, "Thanks, Nanner."

"Anytime Boss."

Spatch looked up at the rest of the crew and smiled, "I hung on as long as I possibly could, but then I couldn't anymore."

"You weren't the weakest link," Clover said.

"Just the opposite in fact. Thank you Spatch, you really came through for us." Cody said.

Cody quickly got up, shook himself off, and immediately began directing the dogs. "Okay Turk and Mop, you need to angle that arbor drone better, so as to redirect the water towards the fire."

"How do we do that?" Mop barked. "The current is striking dead center in the middle of the drone."

"You're going to have to work together and get it lifted up somehow so that the water will blast *away* from the tower towards the fire."

Turk and Marsha joined Mop and all three lifted up one side of the drone, but their legs were shaking wildly.

"With the water crashing down, it's too heavy! We can't hold it!" Turk yelled.

That's when Dagmar and Buford ran over and under the lifted side of the drone.

"Now you schlowly lower it onto usch ant vee'll usen our bodies to keepen it propped up." Dagmar said.

"Won't it crush you?" Mop asked.

"Asch big asch me unt Buford are? No vaaay."

The three dogs slowly lowered it, but towards the end, Marsha scooted under the upended side too. She used her musculature to help lift the side up even higher. Together, the

Pit bull, the Great Dane, and the Newfoundland had created a "pup-tent," using the combined force of their strong bodies to redirect the powerful current of water.

"Just a little higher." Cody urged them on.

The dogs – now unified into a formidable force – pushed their backs deeper into the tent, raising their side of the arbor drone even higher. The current now surged horizontally through the air into the heart of the blazing fire.

A warm cloud of steam billowed up as the fire was doused. Yet thick patches of fire still burned to both the left and right of this section.

"Copper, Maisey, and Kelly, now grab the current with your drone and send it over to the left." Cody barked urgently to his friends.

The dogs quickly rolled their drone into the path of the current and sent it soaring over to the burning trees on the left, extinguishing them in minutes.

"Roxie, Dozer, and Samson, you're next."

The dogs pushed their drone into the path of the left-pointing current.

"Now angle it to the right, so it thoroughly drenches the last of the fire."

The dogs did so and in no time the fire was drowned out into nothing but steaming embers.

"We rock." Cody said. *"Every single one of us.* The fire never even made it across the service path.

# Chapter 29

# A Crushing Defeat

A BRISK WIND cleared the steam and all the bedraggled dogs' eyes narrowed together as Chinny Finster was now revealed in the background, attempting to reactivate one of the defused bombs. The corporate scumbag was too caught up in his deviltry to even notice them.

"Slabfork and Gage, will you please help me offer our friend a nice cool drink?" Cody asked.

The Doberman and St. Bernard grinned from ear to ear, only too happy to oblige. The powerful current was now shot directly at Finster, knocking the scoundrel clean off his feet. With sharp nods of his head, Cody directed the rest of the dogs to surround their adversary. The dogs raised their hackles and gnashed their teeth as Chinny feebly looked around for a chance to escape. The pack quickly formed a tight circle around Finster, who was still on the ground covered in mud.

"Well, look what we have here gang." Cody barked, as he broke through the circle and approached the lost man. "A pig in a puddle."

Finster looked up, somewhat disoriented, and grunted. He looked down at his own hands.

"Those bombs will NOT be reignited Finster." Cody said. "And reducing this orchard to nothing but smoldering ashes? Well, clearly that's not going to happen either. *On your feet parasite.*"

Finster only gave a fiendish grin as he wiped some muck off his face and clamored to regain his balance. "It's only a temporary reprieve *dog*. Despite your best efforts, will we keep fracking this entire country, this entire world for every single last dime we can squeeze out of it. And sooner or later Timberton will be fracked too."

"Really?" Cody asked. "Is that your only intention? *Move.*"

With gnashing teeth and snarling growls the pack led the stumbling Finster back over to the water tower.

"Are you sure you don't want to change your ways?" Cody asked.

"*HELL NO.*" Finster said with utter defiance. "I'll never change. Who cares about your drinking water? Or your fertile soil? Or even your breathable air? There's money to be made, damn it!"

His bulky frame pressed up against the water tower, the dogs now had him cornered. That crackling sound rose up again, except this time it was louder.

"Money isn't everything, you monster." Cody said. "People need safe, clean water. To drink. To bathe in. To give their plants and gardens. To swim..."

"To hell with all that!" Chinny yelled.

*SNAP!*

Another leg of the water tower gave under the strain of Finster's weight and the entire structure violently shifted. A thunderous metallic scraping was heard as the entire tank fell from the top of the tower...

*SQUISH!*

...and landed on top of Chinny Finster, crushing the lower half of his body. Thick viscous bile oozed from his mouth, as he lay there pinned to the ground. A few last rivulets trickled from the tower's drainage valve. The tank was now on it bolt-encrusted curved side, crushing the filth right out of Finster. A rutabaga grub camping out in his belly button popped out and now scowled, realizing its vacation had been cut short.

"Ruh...ruh..." Finster moaned.

*"Ruff?"* Cody asked.

"Ruh..Rul..Roll it off me."

"If we do, will you promise to stop fracking? Not just here, but everywhere?" Cody asked, perhaps a little too hopeful.

"Neh...ver, *never.*" Finster responded, still defiant and unjust as ever.

"Well, that's too bad pal. See, us dogs all know a trick that we're usually taught right from puppyhood. Unfortunately for you, we never forget that trick either. Do we gang?" Cody asked his comrades.

"NO!" they answered.

"Wahh...wha..what's that?" Finster croaked.

"It's not roll-off, it's ROLL-*OVER*!" Cody barked.

All the dogs got behind the huge round water tank and began to push at it until it finally began to slowly roll over the venal slob.

"WAIT!" Spatchcock barked and the dogs stopped rolling over.

Finster gargled and bubbled, slurping at the air trying to catch his breath. The water tank was now up to his chest, the rest of his body flattened like a pancake.

"Isn't this a little cruel?" the frisky Chihuahua said, licking his chops.

"What's that?" Cody asked.

"Leaving all those sweet, crispity, crunchity fingernails on him when clearly they could still be of some use."

Cody looked at Finster's corny claws and then over at the clatch of smaller dogs (most of them with their front paws flat on the ground and their haunches raised up, tails wagging) staring at the fingernails with wide-eyed wonder and drooling tongues lolling out of their little furry pie holes. Finally he smiled.

"Well, alright then. Waste not, want not." Cody consented, making a quick nod.

The smaller dogs bum-rushed Chinny's hands, scarfing down those delectable salty crunchity fingernails in seconds flat, chip dust clinging to their slobbery chops. (World's quickest manicure.)

"Mmm..." they all murmured in unison.

Snack time was over.

"One last chance Finster." Cody said. "Cease and desist with the fracking or kiss what's left of your horrible self good-bye."

"NE-E-E-VER-R-R-R!" the inhuman slob gurgled, sticking out his nasty deformed purple tongue, his last act of defiance.

"Hey Copper, you big old sled-dog you, what's the word I'm thinking of?" Cody barked.

"*MUSH!*" Copper barked right back.

With a final heaving push (and a jolly display of community spirit) all the dogs rolled the water tank over, squishing Chinny into a nasty pulp, a radioactive marmalade of sorts. The pack of furry warriors howled in victory.

Chinny's flattened limbs twitched as McDeath swooped in to claim the foul basterd. Mangled and maimed, squished and squashed, Finster croaked hot blood out of his gaping piehole, intent on spewing even just a little more venom. But in the end he could only mouth the words. Fore – deflated by death – barely a tongue's worth of syllables could surf his last breath. An "Arrrrr..." creaked out before infinite stillness muted him.

The Grim Reaper found Finster so repugnant; he paused to first rub some mentholated ointment under his bony nostril slits (so as to mask the putrid stench). Opening his mouth to smile (he would've licked his chops if he'd still had his tongue -

and any lips), McDeath slipped on a pair of bright yellow dishwashing gloves – pulling them all the way up to his knobby elbows. Finally prepared, he seized the dead demon's soul (believe it or not, he did have one) and flew away to find the nearest rotting station.

"Cooper, you better call for a meat wagon," Cody said, looking at the grisly aftermath of Chinny's stinking remains. "Tell 'em to bring some shovels, hoses, and maybe some hazmat gear too."

Some of the less finicky dogs (who'd missed out on the fingernail feeding frenzy) lingered while the pack departed. Once the coast was clear, they turned back to the steaming pile of gunky smithereens that once filled the Chinny Goblin. Pouring liberally from a bottle of tangy steak sauce, the beasties chowed down on the putrid entrails like a flock of furry vultures, creating a lighter burden for the clean-up crew.

Two of the dogs (who shall remain unnamed) even played tug-a-war with one of the Chinny Goblin's intestines between them, stretching it out like a sausagey rubber band before it snapped, splattering them with a rancid coat of bile and feces.

"Ewww...and they call *me* disgusting," Smokey cringed, as he felt his gorge rise.

## Chapter 30

# Cody Loves Rumblebarry Pie

"IT IS MY distinguished honor today to help inaugurate a new tradition into our fine community." Mayor Hoovenhauer spoke. "From now on, all the dogs in Timberton can eagerly look forward to the third Sunday of each month. For that is when - right here on Kelsey Avenue - all the cobblestone crockery will be placed lovingly down on the street, each holding a heaping slice of rumblebarry pie! Our heroic canines will be forever remembered for having helped us all to come to our senses."

Radiant sunshine blasted from the sky, casting the autumnal color (now at its peak) in a fiery warm glow. A furry dervish approached from the south. Cody led the frack-attack pack of hungry dogs through the city of Timberton, barking loudly for the rest to keep up. The barking frenzy, the scurrying of furry paws, and the drooling doggie tongues surged through the city as the dogs made a mad dash for Kelsey Avenue.

"Let's hear a big welcome for our heroes today!" the mayor exclaimed as the dogs turned the corner onto Kelsey Avenue. A swell of applause greeted them as the Timbertonians cheered.

All along the cobblestone street, people stood at their porches, each holding up two plates of mouthwatering rumblebarry pie. Within mere seconds, the dogs were standing right in front of them, eagerly sniffing at the rumblebarry pie. Cody's beefy tongue went all lickity liver over his slobbery chops.

"Before these tokens of our appreciation are devoured," Hoovenhauer said. "I must make a very important announcement."

Dogs and humans alike turned to their mayor to listen.

"From this day on, fracking is *officially* banned in Timberton!"

Everybody cheered wildly.

"We thank Cody and his friends for fighting so hard to stop the damage to our environment the fracking would've caused. The money wouldn't have lasted, but NOW our WATER, our SOIL, our AIR, and our HEALTH will. And for that, we are eternally grateful to our furry friends."

Another round of applause and cheers.

"Now, please serve our friends their just desserts."

And the Timbertonians set each plate before each dog, humbly saying, "Thank-you" as they did.

Aunt Vivian and Timmy set down a plate of pie for Cody, crouching down next to him. Timmy hugged the chocolate lab with deep gratitude. Cody placed a paw in his little hand and Timmy squeezed it.

"Thank you for remembering what I almost forgot." Aunt Vivian said as she caressed the rich brown fur atop Cody's head.

"I don't know Viv, I saw you at the town meeting and I gotta say: you didn't seem to forget a thing." Cody said. She hugged him a little tighter.

Cody licked both of their faces as his tail wagged, "It's love is all. Never giving up on it. Never questioning it. Never taking it for granted."

*"UNCONDITIONAL LOVE!"* Timmy and Aunt Vivian cheered.

"YES!" Cody said, bringing his snout down to the dish.

The dogs dove into their pie with wolfish appetites and scarfed it down in no time. Some even licked the blue plates clean, checking twice for any missed spots of juice. Then – with purple stained snouts - the dogs all collectively bowed in honor of the generous townsfolk and barked a big, happy, "THANK YOU!" The Timbertonians smiled in return, waved goodbye and said, "YOU'RE WELCOME!" as they removed the plates and watched the dogs run back home.

Sooner than they (or you) could imagine, the horrible misbegotten era of fossil fuel production/extraction would end. Taking root, vast green and infinite sources of renewable energy would take its place.

The Timbertonians had been inspired by the dogs' great valor and wisdom, so much so they were emboldened to take action. Through a series of eco-minded adaptations they changed their town for the better, until it was run on one hundred percent green energy. With a relentless outpouring of love and enthusiasm, the community's participation reached new heights as a hands-on educational system was implemented.

Revolving groups of citizens would work at different sites for intervals of two weeks so as to earn and learn simultaneously. At the Recycling Site they'd learn about biomass and how to utilize the landfill's gases to generate electricity. Then they would move on to Community Gardening where they would learn about carbon sequestration, natural filtration systems, and pollination, which would lead to growing kelp forests, creating bioswales, apiculture, etc. At the Renewable Energy Site they would learn about wind harness maintenance, solar panel manufacturing, and wave energy converters.

Getting into the swing of things himself, old Farmer Redfox began incorporating crop rotation, permaculture, hydroponics, natural animal raising, and other green methods into his own system of sustainable agriculture. At Gorky's behest, he made his farm a designated site, so all Timbertonians could learn and earn too. After all, Redfox was more than capable of giving a "hoot" as well.

As they repeatedly returned to all these sites, the citizens not only earned a healthy wage, but earned a powerful knowledge about all the interconnections of a truly sustainable system. It was an awesome feeling, living a balanced life within Nature herself. Green energy had infinite applications and there were more jobs than there were Timbertonians to fill them. So not only did the town prosper, but it grew as more and more people came to live there.

*And the world would* heal.

# Chapter 31

# Nocturnal Delight

The Timberton dogs trudged through the snow of a cold January night, some of them better built for this arduous task than others. They began to make their way up a large hill, many not sure why.
*Perhaps to howl at the moon?*
Their humans were asleep and none the wiser. Each canine had crept out well after midnight to join the furry procession winding its way through the dark snowy streets and into the wilder outskirts of town. Some wore little doggie sweaters and booties. Many took no notice of the cold, only being too happy to get another chance to frolic in the snow. Two rascally runts made off with Dagmar's scarf so as to play tug-o-war with it. She only smiled.
A million small crunches scraped their ears as their paws broke the icy crisp snow on their way up the hill. Upon reaching the summit they fell into an awed silence at the glorious nocturnal spectacle before them. Their wide-open eyes shone with an ethereal green glow. An emerald aurora's ion curtains rippled through the sky like ribbon candy, an ocean of muted stars swimming it its dreamy translucent waves.

As a refreshing cold breeze washed over the row of dogs perched on the hilltop, they deeply inhaled the fresh air. Tranquility overtaking them, they curled up into a massive mellow fur pile. Together they shared a peaceful communion with the Universe, entranced and alive as they caught the best show on earth.

Cody looked upon his friends, taking in all their wonderment, and smiled.

*Unconditional Love was grand.*

*Illustration by T.L. Stickle*

# Author's Note

When we value human beings only in terms of their economic worth, our intelligence and compassion as a species of a supposedly higher order can easily be brought into question. We are not our jobs, we are not the things we own, and we are not the transient bodies we inhabit for these short lifetimes. We are energy which is constantly changing, developing, and learning to express itself. Unlearning prescribed blueprints for success in today's world is essential for the development and nurturing of one's soul.

Once we have shaken ourselves free from these lazy trappings, we can finally see ourselves, each other, and the world in a whole new light. We Must Learn to Cohabitate with and Honor Mother Earth and never try to dominate Her. Because when we abuse Her, we condemn ourselves. That's when we've lost our deep connection to Nature. We ourselves are Nature, so in a sense we lose ourselves.

Fortunately, that connection can be reestablished. The natural world is not only worthy of our protection, but of our deepest reverence.

After all, nothing lasts forever...and some things are gone too soon.

*Honor Her.*
With Much Love,
Timothy Stickle

*Photo Collage by T.L. Stickle*

# THE DAY AFTER TOMORROW IS
## *THREE DAYS AFTER YESTERDAY*

*There's No More Time For Resistance To Real Change*

*No More Time to Waste*
TIME IS RUNNING out as a deadline begins to coil around our necks and maybe instead of a good nudge, we just need a friendly shove? On the plus side, it's running out for the whole misbegotten (and very dirty) fossil fuel era as well. Oil, natural gas, coal, etc. are finite resources and are not renewable. So, much as the fossil fuel industry can't stand to admit it, time simply isn't on their side. They will run dry, there's no escaping that. Unfortunately for the rest of us it won't happen soon enough.

But if we do reach that moment in time, we will all collectively cringe as they predictably and very hypocritically start selling us green energy (*insert vomiting emoticon right here). Let's hope we never forget how willingly they subverted our political system for the sake of their insatiable greed and wanton degradation of our environment. The massive amounts of destruction they've inflicted through their offshore drilling, fracking, tar sands, leaking pipelines, mountain top removals, etc. is unforgivable. Let's hope they're never given an opportunity to finally change *only* when they had no other choice.

*Change Can't Come Quick Enough*
Ultimately all of us will have to fully embrace renewable sources of energy. Not even our most venal retrograde pollies (who couldn't care less about future generations) will be able to stop the change coming, which is inevitable. They can deny science now in favor of profits, but history will judge them accordingly. Peoples' lives have been irreparably damaged because of their criminal negligence and complicity.

Wind, Solar, Hydro, Biomass, and Geothermal Power have already been successfully adopted by many forward-thinking countries like Costa Rica. The United Kingdom employs offshore windfarms to generate most of its electricity now as it progresses in lowering its carbon emissions. All of us should be aiming for carbon-neutrality. Unfortunately in America, over two thirds of our energy still comes from fossil fuels. This is because corporate hucksters masquerading as upright politicians have not only infiltrated our system, but have completely overtaken it, ensuring Big Oil's dominance over our energy production. All while casually endangering peoples' lives with their reckless pollution and unethical business practices.

*Water Scarcity*
With the United Nations predicting a global water shortage of 40% by 2030 – let me repeat that, *A GLOBAL WATER SHORTAGE OF 40% BY 2030*, we need to kick these nasty clowns to the curb. We can't afford their devastation to our water sources and environment, not a second longer. Water scarcity needs to be addressed *now*. Millions of lives could be lost if we fail to act.

I won't lie. I AM ANGRY. I'm inconsolably disappointed and disillusioned by our venal political system and federal agencies. Waxing proleptic, I'm sure my detractors will write this book off as mere "green propaganda" full of infantile allegories and hoary ad hominems. Yet too many of us already know the ugly truth and just how dire the reality of our broken system truly is. Regardless, check the bibliography: facts are facts.

*Reconnecting with Nature*

Nature is essential nourishment, sort of a holistic magic where your sense of home is reinforced whenever you're reminded of the living breathing world you're a part of. You are spoken to, and you speak back. Through this ancient communication intrinsic knowledge is tapped into and from there you're helpless but to revel in the existential freedom and peace that is YOU.

When humans disregard Nature they are in effect denying a deeper part of themselves. If this vital connection is broken, chaos and destruction soon follow, with domination and exploitation being the most common results. Yet cross HER enough and she will not only defend herself, but she will retaliate.

Human follies abound! There is much fertile ground to be plowed. So please my friends, allow your minds some room to breathe. Come and feast on some deliciously dark dissent until you too are wonderfully out of sync with the world (and *business as usual*).

If we act out of LOVE and a vibe of sweet urgency, then maybe we can rev up this transition into a better world and actually arrive just in time.

But, if we fail to act...well, let me offer a bit of black humor:

*-What did the Executioner say to the Calendar just before carrying out his sentence?*

*-"Your days are numbered."*

Much (Bittersweet) Love,
Timothy Stickle

# FRACKING ABSURD

*The Promise of "Energy Independence" Is an Empty One*

*Fracking: A Controversial Method of Fossil Fuel Extraction*
Shale regions (Marcellus, Eagle Ford, Bakken, etc.) around the United States are being drilled for their natural gas (which is primarily methane), often falsely claimed a "clean" alternative to coal. This process is known as fracking/hydraulic fracturing - a controversial method of fossil fuel extraction – wherein horizontal drilling curves into the shale formations to create wells. The pressurized injection of massive amounts of water mixed with sand and a blend of toxic chemicals (benzene, toluene, formaldehyde, etc.) are then used to fracture the porous rock, releasing the natural gas.

The gas then makes its way back up with some of the fracking fluid. Before the gas is sold to consumers it is purified in compressor stations. There VOCs are vented from their relief valves right into the air. Afterward, the toxic filth that is fracking fluid/wastewater (2.5 billion gallons are produced in the USA *every day*) is either stored in pits or shot into deep-injection wells.

Sounds pretty clean, huh? What could possibly go wrong?

*Dangerous and Dirty*
A lot as it turns out, because fracking is a dangerous and unnecessary business. Drilling waste is buried around watersheds. Groundwater is contaminated with endocrine cycle-disrupting chemicals. Massive gas leaks cause evacuations of neighborhoods. Blowouts release thousands of gallons of toxic flowback. Manufacturing water scarcity, fracking is often

allowed to continue unabated in drought stricken areas (even though the sheer amount of water needed to create a gigajoule is ridiculous).

Next, whether it's in California or Pennsylvania, aquifers are often threatened when wastewater is injected into deep wells (with casings that leak), potentially contaminating drinking water. Earthquakes have resulted from wastewater disposal wells too (Kansas, Ohio, Oklahoma, etc.). Consequently, fracking leaves in its wake the blight of industrial wastelands full of sacrifice zones.

Additionally natural gas/methane is a powerful greenhouse gas even better than carbon dioxide at trapping heat in our atmosphere. Also, some of it leaks from the wells, perhaps as much as 6%. This contributes to climate change just like the burning of coal. So it's a false solution, which in reality just exacerbates old problems.

*Halliburton Loophole Exemptions*

Big Oil & Gas are very similar to Big Tobacco, in that they go to extreme lengths to hide their incriminating evidence, while publicly claiming their product is safe. Halliburton created fracking back in 1949. Dick Cheney was the CEO of Halliburton from 1995 to 2000. As Vice President, Cheney would help create the Energy Policy Act of 2005. This gave the fracking industries exemptions to the Clean Air Act, the Clean Water Act, and the Safe Drinking Water Act. This act, commonly known as the "Halliburton Loophole," is a bastardized use of American legislation to serve corporate interests. If fracking were truly safe, why did they create/need all the exemptions to environmental safety regulations?

The people (some duped, some very willing) who sign lease agreements for Big Oil & Gas to frack their land are often ripped off. Their royalty checks also sucked dry by "new" expenses. Transportation costs, vague gathering fees, blatant lies regarding the amounts of gas collected are just some of them. The landowners soon discover just how deceptive (and insatiably greedy) the oil and gas companies are. They hide profits, obfuscate their myriad deductions, use intentionally ambiguous contractual language, operate with little to no regulatory oversight, and so on.

*Feeling Fracked*

So not only is the environment fracked, but so are many of the landowners who sold their mineral rights. When these greedy behemoths try to rip off the government (which they do attempt to do, as leases are also sold on federal lands), the government has many resources to recoup the *billions* of royalty payments stolen. Yet for the average landowner, paying thousands for auditing and/or arbitration just isn't a reality. They need to do some serious homework before getting into bed with those wolves.

With green energy being capable of giving us all the power we need, why is this dirty business still happening? (Obvious answers: Big Oil & Gas, their lobbyists, venal pollies on the take, etc.) We're continuously careless with our water. Thus, I can't help but wonder if water scarcity is part of a bigger (and even more insidious) plan. Is fracking laying the tracks toward water privatization?

- Much Love (and distress), T. Stickle

# PLASTIC (NOTSO) FANTASTIC

*Innovative Activists Take on Our Plastic Waste Crisis*

*Finding plastic pollution solutions is a priority*
The world uses a trillion plastic shopping bags every year. The world buys a million plastic bottles every minute of every hour of every single day. Eight million tons of plastic waste wind up in our oceans every year. In fact, with the world producing over 330,000,000 metric tons of plastic every year (50% of which is used only once and then thrown away) plastic pollution is a major problem on many levels.

Plastics in the ocean pose multiple threats. Thousands of marine animals are entangled and drowned by plastic refuse. When these plastics break down into microplastics they often combine with other pollutants which are then fed on by many marine creatures. That poison can build up into lethal amounts, unfortunately contaminating their milk. Consequently they can wind up killing their own offspring. Dead sea animals are being found in increasing numbers on beaches with stomachs full of plastic waste. As for all the marine life consuming microplastics – as it works its way up the food chain – we don't as of yet have any major studies on the effects of this pollution on humans.

I'm betting it can't be good.

*Innovative Solutions to Fighting Plastic Pollution*
On the positive side there is a growing response to plastic pollution around the world. Some cities are banning bottled water and straws, there are firms striving to create truly biodegradable plastic. As mindfulness transforms into action,

young activists are becoming increasingly creative in their approaches to this problem.

In August 2017, brothers Gary and Sam Bencheghib paddled through toxic filth down the Citarum River (widely considered the world's most polluted river) in Indonesia in two kayaks made from plastic bottles. Gary had formed his own company called Make a Change World, which focuses on creating video projects about pollution's effects on our world, using social media to spread the word. At a younger age he had witnessed a favorite swimming spot in Bali turning into a plastic dumping site. The environmental degradation deeply affecting him.

They set out to create a series of videos which would hopefully inspire others to care for the environment (and realize just how intense plastic pollution has become). They used plastic bottles to help build their kayaks to show that plastic can still be a valuable resource (after its initial use). The videos of their two-week trip paddling down the Citarum were so successful the Indonesian government responded promptly and pledged to create a rehabilitation program for the river.

### Taking on the Great Pacific Garbage Patch

Boyan Slat and his Ocean Cleanup project are aiming at no less than clearing all the oceans of plastic by 2050. His first target is the Great Pacific Garbage Patch. This floating concentration of trash (mostly plastic) in the North Pacific Ocean, reportedly twice the size of Texas. Slat launched his fleet of giant floating booms, which collected and funneled the garbage to a central tank. Sea Anchors which float deep in the ocean will helped keep the booms mobile, along with gyres and deep-water tides.

Slat says this endeavor is very time-sensitive because the plastic must be collected before it breaks down into dangerous microplastics. After some technical difficulties with his booms, Slat switched his focus to how plastic is entering the oceans to begin with, which is mainly from extremely polluted rivers. This brought on the creation of his Interceptors, solar-powered trash collection barges which use the rivers' natural currents to "close the tap" before the rivers' plastic refuse can reach the oceans.

*Making Waves*

I'm impressed these young activists are addressing the consequences of our global plastic pollution. Where federal agencies have dropped the ball (due to being controlled by the very industries they're supposed to be overlooking), the Bencheghib brothers and Slat are just some of the many activists helping to fill the void. Significantly they're very adept at reaching people and communicating with them on an intimate level. Solutions are needed now more than ever, especially with the dearth of real leadership in the world today.

I feel some hope knowing young people – outside of the system – are still striving towards a viable future, especially when so many have sadly deemed it a lost cause.

- Much Love, T. Stickle

# STANDING ROCK #NODAPL

### A SLAPP to the Face

*Stopping Fossil Fuel Development*
The Sioux's concerns for their water and sacred grounds were ignored by the corporate interests involved. Yet millions of people around the world heard them loud and clear: stopping fossil fuel development is a global priority. We have no time left for the insatiable greed of the fossil fuel industry. And as they paint humanity into a corner, we have no room left for denial of the dire situation we're all facing.

In May 2014, ETP (Energy Transfer Partners) decided to build the Dakota Access Pipeline, to transfer oil from the Bakken shale oil fields in North Dakota down to Illinois. The original planned route had the pipeline crossing underneath the Missouri River near Bismarck. It was rejected by the US-ACE (the United States Army Corps of Engineers) because it ran too close to municipal waters. With blatant disregard for the Treaty of Fort Laramie, it was rerouted a half mile from the Standing Rock Indian Reservation.

*Pipelines Threaten Rivers*
Continued fossil fuel development this late in the game is backwards thinking period, but it shows the relentless self-serving interests of Big Oil. Their false claims of improvements to public safety and that we can achieve "energy independence" by building more and more pipelines are laughable at best. Less than six months after the DAPL was operational, the Keystone Pipeline leaked more than 400,000 gallons (*not* 210,000 gallons) of oil in South Dakota.

If we remember all the other rivers (Kalamazoo River, Yellowstone River, etc.) devastated by faulty pipelines, wanting to vigorously protect the Missouri River makes perfect sense. Big Oil epitomizes the dark side of capitalism. Regardless of how many times they painfully sully our environment, they manage to thrive as they wield formidable control of our political system. Rigging the game in their favor, they receive billions of dollars in subsidies, reap billions of dollars in profit. They inflict horrendous damage on our environment (yet remain unscathed for their crimes).

*Message Amplified*

The protests near the Standing Rock Indian Reservation drew attention from around the world. A few hundred water protectors quickly turned into thousands and camps (Sacred Stone and Oceti Sakowin) were created to accommodate them. Many woke people immediately recognized the situation for what it was: another case of corporations and the government disrespecting indigenous people (and their treaty rights) for the sake of profit. The massive resistance generated by the Standing Rock #NoDAPL movement gave ETP a serious headache. They retaliated by launching a campaign to intimidate the protestors (and future ones).

ETP did many reprehensible things during Standing Rock #NoDAPL, but having a law firm file a bogus racketeering complaint against BankTrack (*a divestment group), Greenpeace, and Earth First for $300 million with information gathered by TigerSwan, a private security firm they hired, was un-American in its design to suppress free speech/dissent. It's a SLAPP (a strategic lawsuit against public participation) which uses expensive litigation to suppress free speech. The ultimate point isn't to win the suit. It's to intimidate potential dissenters who might dare object to their reckless (and hellishly unethical) business practices.

Thankfully we have this thing called the First Amendment and many states are passing anti-SLAPP legislation to help "slap" these corporate pigs back into reality.

### Buying Their Own Army

Protecting their interests, ETP supplied police with various equipment and $15 million for "law enforcement expenses," in effect buying their own militarized police force. Many reports abound of the police using unwarranted force on protestors. This included tear gas, rubber bullets, attack dogs, water and sound cannons, etc. Jumping into the fray, over 2,000 veterans came to Standing Rock to act as a "human shield" between the water protectors and the police. It was a beautiful act of respect and peace, a moment of graceful compassion not soon to be forgotten.

The pipeline might have been finished, but the inspiration generated by the Standing Rock movement will be felt for years to come. More people are aware about the inherent dangers of unnecessary pipelines and despite all the intimidation tactics employed, are more emboldened than ever to scrutinize (and fight) them from being installed in their communities.

*Standing together counts.*

-Much Love, T. Stickle

# THE FLINT WATER CRISIS

### Your Water Is Safe To Drink

*Failing to Protect the Public*

In a reckless decision (originally thought to be a cost-saving measure) in April 2014, Flint's water source was switched from Detroit Water/Lake Huron to the Flint River (temporarily while the KWA pipeline was being constructed). With many of the city's old lead pipes dating back to the early twentieth century, and a bizarre lack of corrosion controls in the (un)treatment of the raw river water, outbreaks of lead poisoning and Legionnaires' disease weren't exactly unforeseeable results. That said it still took a hell of a long time until anybody *would* see.

Regardless of a steady stream of complaints about the tainted water from the citizens of the poorest city in America, the MDHHS (Michigan Department of Health and Human Services), the MDEQ (Michigan Department of Environmental Quality), Governor Rick Snyder, and a host of other state and federal agencies and employees turned a deaf ear on them. (*Well, not everybody was ignored: when General Motors complained about how corrosive the water was, they got hooked right back up to the safe water, while the public was left to flounder in filthy Flint River water. *Cha-ching!*)

With criminal negligence, these culprits refused to acknowledge the burgeoning public health crisis, provided false assurances (despite being aware of the contamination) along with bogus testing methods/results, and dragged their feet with resistance while the public remained in jeopardy. Snyder knew about the lead contamination for a year and a half, but couldn't have cared less about all the children he was endangering. At least until enough bad press and the national spotlight pulled them out of their reluctance. *Then* they were a little more cooperative.

*What was the cost of their greed, negligence, and incompetence?*

*Paying for Someone Else's Mistakes*

Besides all the usual resignations, firings, and lawsuits, the consequences for the innocent were/are dire. Perhaps over one hundred thousand people exposed to lead poisoning, at least ten thousand of them children - who could exhibit multiple severe health problems in the future. Over eighty people contracted Legionnaires' disease and twelve people have been killed by it so far. Decreased fertility for women and increased fetal deaths. And so on.

Yes, those aged lead pipes are finally being replaced with new water service lines in thousands of homes throughout Flint and supposedly the public will be notified more "promptly" if another impending disaster should ever occur. We can only hope. The prolonged negligence toward the Flint Water Crisis even makes the response time to Hurricane Katrina look speedy. Racism and classism rear their ugly heads often when it comes to helping impoverished American cities which have predominantly poc populations.

*Who Can You Trust?*

It's a painful reminder any system is only as good as the people entrusted to run it. Venal pollies and bureaucratic zombies need to be cast out, especially where the public's welfare is concerned. Ain't it kinda kooky: Nestlé gets to pay a mere $200/year to suck up over 130 million gallons of Michigan's water every year (then selling it right back to us for billions of dollars of profit) while Flint was left to suffer because somebody "up there" decided paying $100/day for the anti-corrosive additive for the river water was just too high a price ($1.5 billion in damages looks a lot worse I bet). Let's hope a day of reckoning catches up to all who made that corruption possible.

*Those Who Did Care*

I have to give a shout-out to a few beautiful souls who really made a difference: LeeAnne Walters, Miguel Del Toral, Dr. Mona Hanna-Attisha, Curt Guyette, Melissa Mays and Dr. Marc Edwards. And a big shout-out to all of the people who got out every day to serve their community by delivering clean water, keeping their neighbors informed, and simply helping each other get through the whole hellish ordeal. Your tremendous spirit and perseverance is an inspiration.

When so many agencies and elected officials failed to live up to their responsibilities, honorable people like you took up the slack. So when I'm down and out and find my faith in humanity wavering, I think of folks like you (and feel a little more hopeful).

- Much Love, T. Stickle

# HEAD FOR THE HILLS

*Climate Gentrification Emerges as a New Threat*

### Sea Levels Rising

Sea level rise (stoked by glacial melt, ice sheet loss, and thermal expansion), is accelerating according to satellite data measurements and tide gauges. It is now causing regular nuisance flooding in Miami-Dade County and a direct consequence is the rapid appreciation of higher-elevation properties. While beach-front property is losing a lot of its appeal and thus facing depreciation, black neighborhoods like Little Haiti and Liberty City are located at higher elevations and are thus becoming more coveted for the security they provide.

Unfortunately these communities could be displaced and priced out of their own neighborhoods as their land increases in value. Ho Chi Minh City, New York, Tokyo, London, Mumbai, Washington D.C., etc. (many of which are experiencing chronic flooding) are all at high risk from sea level rise now and in the near future (up to two feet of sea-level rise is predicted globally by the end of this century).

### Wildfires Burning Out of Control

Sea level rise however, is only one consequence of global warming which feeds into climate gentrification. With over a hundred people killed, almost two million acres and 20,000 homes burned up by well over eight thousand different fires, and over $3.5 billion in damages, California experienced a catastrophic wildfire season in 2018, the worst ever recorded there in fact. People living in fire prone areas are more likely to relocate than rebuild due to lack of insurance, which in turn will put pressure on low-income communities as their land appreciates due to its relative safety.

Then there are extreme temperature hikes. In Arizona, Phoenicians are flocking up north to Flagstaff (sometimes as much as forty degrees cooler) so as to escape the oppressive heat (120 degrees at times), but the town is reeling (and unprepared) for such massive amounts of people which is severely increasing housing costs. This is one small example of the climate migration which is becoming pervasive in America today. Canada will soon want to build its own wall to keep northbound Americans out.

### Super Storms Abound

Then extreme weather events like Hurricanes Katrina (over 1,800 people killed/$125 billion in damages), Sandy (over 230 people killed/$70 billion in damages), Harvey (over 105 people killed/$125 billion in damages), and Maria (over 3,050 people killed/$90 billion in damages) are increasing in both frequency and intensity. Tens of thousands of people are displaced. Where will they all go? Climate change refugees abound as they are forced to search for new inhabitable homes. Sadly this phenomenon is more likely to be seen as a field day for opportunistic real estate investors than as a humanitarian crisis of staggering proportions, which it is first and foremost.

### Being Reactive Isn't Enough

With many venal pollies being paid to be climate change deniers, business as usual goes on for the fossil fuel industry, leaving millions of people threatened on multiple levels. While most would agree we're woefully unprepared for the savage consequences of global warming, some measures are being taken: seawalls are being built, green development in some cities is underway, fire-resistant building materials are beginning to be subsidized by the government, controlled burnings to reduce the fuel of wildfire outbreaks, etc.

Yet reinforcing things to be more resilient for the next round of disasters is not enough by far. We need to fundamentally change how we live and honestly address *the causes* of our current predicaments if we wish to continue life on Earth.

- Much Love, T. Stickle

# GOING OFF THE RAILS

*The Ohio Toxic Train Derailment*

*Whittling Away Safety Measures*

You would think the railroad companies would be eager to avoid a toxic train derailment. But if doing so interferes with their profits, they're just not too gung-ho. Used by most American railroads, PSR (precision scheduled railroading) is a business philosophy/operational model which focuses on cost-saving measures at the expense of safety. For the sake of hyper efficiency, they keep the trains running for as long as possible, and with as little downtime as possible. But downtime is when the trains are supposed to be inspected. Under this foolhardy plan – which values shareholders over stakeholders - over 40% of equipment maintenance workers were cut, and over 20,000 railroad workers were laid off in 2019 alone. This is why inspection times have been so drastically cut.

Carmen, the freight car mechanics who are responsible for the train's safety, are extremely frustrated because they no longer have the time to properly inspect the train cars. It usually was only two minutes to start with, but now that time has been cut by 75% down to less than thirty seconds. Not only is this very risky, but it's impossible too. So the train companies are now having the trains inspected before they even hit the rail yard by the train crew. This is completely inappropriate because they're not qualified to perform them. They do this because carmen are specifically required to perform them unless they're not available. So they set up this rudimentary pit stop just to save a little money and time.

In response the FRA (Federal Railroad Administration) sent letters to the rail companies' CEOs, asking them not to take advantage of that loophole, and to actually perform the safety inspections. But they didn't listen, nor did they have to. This is because of regulatory capture, which is when the industry being regulated is more powerful than the regulators.

*Paving the Way Towards Disaster*
Then there's increasing train lengths. Between 2008 and 2017, the average train length was 75 cars. The FRA classifies a train of 150 cars (1.9miles long) as "very long." And the GAO (Government Accountability Office) has stated that some trains are even three miles long now. And it's not uncommon for crews as tiny as only two rail workers to be operating these behemoths.

Obama's administration wanted trains carrying tons of hazardous materials to start using an ECP (electronically controlled pneumatic brakes) system which brakes all the cars simultaneously; instead of the Civil War-era braking system (which is a car-by-car braking system) still used today. The rail companies performed some major pushback against these new safety measures, lobbying against them. Trump's administration would repeal this requirement in 2018, citing it's high costs.

Considering all that, can it be any wonder there are over 1,000 train derailments a year?

*Train Derailment in East Palestine Ohio*
In February of 2023 a Norfolk Southern freight train 1.9 miles/150 cars long and carrying over 1.8 million gallons of waste made its way from Madison, Illinois to Conway, Pennsylvania. Hydrogen chloride, phosgene, butyl acrylate, ethylhexyl acrylate, ethylene glycol monobutyl ether, and vinyl chloride

were some of the hazardous materials being transported in twenty of those cars.

Just over fifty of those cars would derail in East Palestine, Ohio right long the Ohio-Pennsylvania border on February third. Almost 2,000 residents were evacuated within a two mile radius. Hoping to avoid five tank cars from exploding, they burned off 100,000 gallons of vinyl chloride, causing a massive plume of black smoke in America's latest toxic train derailment.

When you burn vinyl chloride, you release dioxins which are incredibly toxic. And those dioxins would travel miles far away from East Palestine, affecting people and other animals with an array of ailments. There were myriad reports of people suffering from severe rashes, coughing, burning eyes, lung problems, etc. Animals have suffered and died too. Many are worried about the vinyl chloride residue as well. Many citizens now want to leave, but their homes have been severely devalued and now they're stuck. We are at the mercy of greedy corporations with no meaningful oversight.

Dubious Concern

Stacking the odds in their favor, Norfolk Southern would hire CTEH(Center for Toxicology and Environmental Health) to do environmental testing. CTEH, known primarily for toxicology monitoring for Big Oil, is notorious for downplaying public health dangers after disasters caused by corporations. From the 2010 BP Deepwater Horizon oil spill (well over 3 million barrels of oil spilled into the ocean), to the toxic coal ash in Tennessee in 2008, CTEH is an industry lapdog, who's paid to provide the results corporations are looking for.

The public's safety is definitely not their priority, but corporate interests most certainly are. Corporations utilize places like CTEH as a part of their disinformation campaigns to help thwart lawsuits, sensible regulation, and other public health protections.

The NTSB (National Transportation Safety Board) is currently conducting an investigation which isn't expected to be completed until March 2024. And that's a good thing. Environmental disasters require time, so as to have the damage properly assessed, to understand the long-term consequences, and hopefully to reflect on mistakes and discover humane solutions.

This is an old story we – the public – know all too well. So what's the cost, the real cost? The $400 million Norfolk Southern lost? The people of East Palestine suffering from having their homes devalued, along with worrying about potential health problems in the future? I think it runs even deeper. I think this latest environmental disaster has a spiritual toll, especially taken along with all the others.

It puts yet another dent in America's reputation. It makes the citizens even more cynical as they witness how our government is essentially controlled by corporations. Perhaps worst of all, it shows how corporations always tend to value money (no matter what the cost) over human life.

It's a very old story...and a very sad one.

Much Love, Tim Stickle

# ACKNOWLEDGEMENTS

Thank You Dearly:

Mom/Marilyn Stickle
Rayna Humason aka the "Silhouette Lady"
Mary Kay Hopkins
Pauline Kurschat
60 Minutes
Dr. Jeffrey Wigand
Molly Ivins
Al Gore
Chris Harris & Molly Litvin
Jewel Thais-Williams
John Muir
Erin Brockovich
Antoinette Tuff
Michael Moore
Agnes Varda
Rob Stewart
Dian Fossey

# GLOSSARY

**agitprop train** – Agitational propaganda usually of a political nature which uses media as its vehicle. The Bolsheviks originally used agitprop in Soviet Russia to help promote the Communist Party.

**albedo effect** – The amount of electromagnetic radiation reflected back into the atmosphere/space compared to that which is absorbed. The more the polar ice sheets/glaciers melt away, the lower the albedo effect drops, resulting in increased global warming.

**ALEC** – The American Legislative Exchange Council is a political lobbying group who writes laws on behalf of corporations. They push extreme policies (e.g. Stand Your Ground) for their own personal profit while bringing harm to everyday people. They're essentially puppeteers for our lawmakers.

**aquifer** – A stratum of permeable rock, gravel, or sand that can contain or transmit water. They typically supply water for wells (ground water). Fracking has led to increased contamination of our ground water/aquifers due to its lack of well integrity, waste water dumping, etc.

**biomimicry** – When humans turn to Nature for inspiration: burrs lead to Velcro, birds lead to airplanes, whales lead to wind turbines, etc. Learning sustainability is one of biomimicry's main benefits.

**bioremediation** – Using microorganisms or plant enzymes to remove environmental pollutants (from soil, water, air, etc.).

**bioswales** – Channels which are designed to filter stormwater by removing pollution via vegetation, mulch, soil, etc.

**carbon emissions** – aka greenhouse gas emissions. The burning of fossil fuels releases carbon emissions (carbon dioxide, ozone, methane, etc.) into our atmosphere where they absorb radiation, which in turn increases global warming. Sources of carbon emissions include: vehicles, wastewater treatment facilities, factories, and fracking.

**change** – To transform into something different; hopefully something better than before. Ideally change is a process of positive personal growth.

**Citizens United** – One of the most heinous decisions ever in America, it gave/gives corporations (in particular the oil and gas industry) tremendous influence over our government and laws. It is blatant corruption – in all its venal ugliness – in broad daylight.

**climate change** – The weather grows increasingly extreme: temperatures skyrocket, glaciers melt away massive amounts of ice, sea-level rise encroaches higher and higher, storms exhibit harsher severity, etc. And many pollies won't even deign to acknowledge it as the all too real life-threatening phenomenon it sadly is.

**climate change deniers** – Most often people who are paid to engender uncertainty in the public by casting doubt on scientific consensus. These venal pollies, conservative media hacks, and other such fossil fuel flunkies perpetuate public disinformation at the behest of the industries they're well paid to serve.

**climate gentrification** – When people (often lower income and/or poc) are priced right out of their own neighborhoods/communities which are now considered ideal geographic areas resistant to climate change (e.g. beachfront property goes underwater, financially and literally, due to accelerated sea level rise, so wealthy people seize upon the higher ground properties, creating a new real estate feeding frenzy).

cloud seeding – Dumping silver iodide crystals into clouds so as to artificially produce more rain. A reaction to climate change.

coalition – Unity and Alliance to create combined Action so as to accomplish a common Goal. The Will of The People Will be Heard.

conservation - Protecting Our Home, Mother Earth. Unfortunately many "humans" out there are cursed with a gross sense of entitlement, thinking they have free reign to simply plunder and exploit our natural environment to no end. Conservationists (John Muir, Dian Fossey, Henry David Thoreau, et al) have struggled throughout history to bring about a heightened awareness of environmental ethics, demonstrating the importance of preserving and protecting our world.

corruption – Sadly this word is now synonymous with most of today's politicians (who have become increasingly venal) and corporations who use their power to acquire even more power and/or benefits for themselves. The current turnstile between huge American corporations and Washington is a perfect example of corruption: they pretend to enter the world of politics with society's best interests in mind, when sadly, they're going in with corporate agendas to carry out. *See the Cheney/Halliburton Loophole.*

gas flaring – When fossil fuels are extracted, gas flaring is used to burn off unwanted gases and/or to relieve pressure from the wells. It releases massive amounts of carbon dioxide into the atmosphere.

**fossil fuels** – Non-renewable carbon-dense fuels (natural gas, coal, oil) derived from the remains of plants and animals buried millions of years ago. These finite sources of energy have contributed greatly to global warming.

**fossil fuel divestment campaigns** – Strategic means (via social, political, and economic pressure) to expedite the renewable energy transition by stigmatizing fossil fuel companies.

**fracking** - Hydraulic fracturing is an unconventional and highly controversial method of fossil fuel extraction. Using horizontal drilling many toxic carcinogenic fluids (e.g. benzene, hydrochloric acid, and ethanol), lots of precious water (up to 7,000,000 gallons per well) and sand are injected under high pressure into bore holes (some over 7,000 feet deep) to fracture porous rock formations (e.g. the Bakken, Marcellus, and Eagle Ford Shales), so as to release tight oil and natural gas. Water contamination and air pollution are two of the most severe threats fracking inflicts upon our environment (although there are others such as earthquakes).

**gag orders/NDA: Non-disclosure agreements** – aka confidentiality agreements. Usually a "legal" contract between two parties which prohibits one of them from sharing protected information with outsiders. It's one of the main tactics corporations employ to handle damage control when they don't want their nasty little secrets known to the wider public. Whistleblowers (heroes like Jeffrey Wigand and Edward Snowden) often defy these so as to alert the public to the dangerous, illegal, and/or dishonest activities occurring in the corporations/organizations they're working for.

**global warming** – A distinct rise in temperature of the Earth's climate system brought on by increased greenhouse gases. Some of the more heinous consequences of global warming are: cataclysmic weather events (hurricanes, tsunamis, droughts, blizzards, etc.), rising sea levels (with a potentially devastating effect of displacing millions of people), increased species extinctions (their delicate ecosystems damaged by dramatic temperature shifts), and ocean acidification.

**greenhouse effect** – Greenhouse gases (e.g. carbon dioxide, methane) created by the burning of fossil fuels (and intense deforestation) build up in our atmosphere and absorb Earth's natural thermal radiation, rather than allowing it to reflect back out into space. This blocked warmth is then re-radiated back down to the surface where people and animals live, raising the temperature and causing *global warming.*

**hucksters** – aka flimflam men and women. A deceptive person who sells things (usually of very low value) in an aggressive and dishonest manner. Most politicians, corporate lobbyists, and many media representatives are hucksters; more often than not well-paid agents of disinformation. When encountering such unsavory characters of that ilk, Knowledge is truly power and one's best defense.

**low-carbon economy** – A fresh start to create a world more resistant to climate change (while simultaneously diminishing it) by continuing the transition to low-carbon sources of energy. The health of the Earth and Her People depends on it.

**microcystins** – Toxins produced by blue-green algae (cyanobacteria). In humans, it tends to do the most damage to the livers, and in wildlife it can often be fatal. Toxic algal blooms teeming with microcystins are usually created by agricultural runoff, wastewater, and other forms of pollution.

**moratorium** – A suspension/prohibition of an activity. New York, for instance, has placed an on-going moratorium on fracking so as to continue studies on all the potential health risks and environmental harm related to the unconventional drilling technique. Science and education on the matter have won out there whereas sadly, so many other states' politicians have acted out of greed and ignorance...and in the process endangered their own constituents by jumping right into the whole mess.

**Mother Earth/Nature** – Essential nourishment for all life. A deep integrationist awareness which allows one to understand they are a part of everything alive and that everything alive is a part of them. To embrace Her is to place oneself in perfect alignment with the Universe. Her heart beats within You and it's life-affirming.

**oxytocin** – Every dog's (and human's) favorite chemical messenger, this "cuddle/snuggle" hormone helps build unconditional love between animals and humans.

**PFAs** – Perfluroroalyl and polyfluoroalkyl substances aka "forever chemicals," are linked to myriad forms of cancer and are DuPont's unfortunate gift to the world.

**phytoremediation** – a bioremediation process which uses mainly plants and trees to clean up and restore contaminated water, air, and soil.

**progress** – Moving and developing forward into something better. Humans leaving behind the fossil fuel era for renewable sources of energy is progress. Although many gas and oil companies are fighting tooth and nail to stifle this progress for their own selfish (economic) interests, they cannot stop such inevitable change.

**renewable energy** - Naturally recurring energy such as solar, hydro, wind, and biomass. Wind farms, hydroelectric dams, photovoltaic (PV) power stations, and stump harvesting are just a few CLEAN & GREEN methods of producing renewable energy and a beautiful way of establishing a harmonious rhythm with Planet Earth. Whereas fossil fuels are a finite resource and damage our environment just to extract them, renewable energies are infinite and beneficial to our environment.

**retrograde** – This is unfortunately where our venal pollies keep us stuck: backwards and sometimes even moving further backwards...all at the behest of their corporate masters. As a result true progress into a sustainable future is obstructed.

**sacrifice zones** – When a geographic area (along with its people) who are permanently harmed via toxic chemical exposure, pollution of their water supply, unregulated dumping of hazardous waste, etc. Many poisoned communities are largely made up of low-income and people of color.

**sustainable farming** – Farming practices that are decidedly nurturing to both the environment and society, rather than exploitative. This approach encompasses (vertical) food forests, animal welfare, avoiding soil erosion, hydroponics, permaculture, urban agriculture, etc.

**sustainability** – This concept has proved increasingly elusive to our current pollies, who essentially are indifferent to the needs of younger/future generations. Their narrow focus on present economic gains leaves younger citizens in the lurch with many compromised and painful days ahead.

**unconditional love** – Love no matter what. Love without conditions. A complete and pure Love regardless of expectations and with no IFs ever involved. The Love a dog gives to its human: a joyous bond that is unchanging and without limitations. A Love that All Humans should extend to Mother Nature, Planet Earth, and of course, to each other.

**VOCs (volatile organic compounds)** – Chemicals with a high vapor pressure such as formaldehyde, benzene, gasoline, xylene, toluene, acetone, etc. Prolonged exposure to them can lead to nausea, nosebleeds, infertility, birth defects, liver and kidney damage, heart attacks and even cancer. These are being vented (from gas wells' relief valves) into our air on a regular daily basis.

**wastewater/flowback fluid** – The "produced"/poisonous water left over from fracking operations. Add NORM (naturally occurring radioactive materials) such as radium and uranium (released from the rock during the drilling process) to the toxic carcinogenic fluids (e.g. benzene, hydrochloric acid, and ethanol) used for fracking and you wind up with this incredibly nasty stew. If and when this liquid fracking waste reaches aquifers (it has even been illegally dumped into aquifers in California), a major contamination of groundwater results. Earthquakes have been linked to the injection of fracking wastewater into the ground, in disposal wells.

**water** – H2O. Essential to all life on Earth. Should be valued and protected much more vigorously, but is taken for granted more often than not. Oil companies have been particularly damaging to water (the Deepwater Horizon/BP oil spill, the Exxon Valdez oil spill, et al).

**waterkeeper** – Crucial citizens who try to protect and maintain the quality of bodies of water…in the face of much adversity.

**watershed** – An area of rivers and streams which drain into larger bodies of water. They need valiant protection as they often feed into our drinking water.

**will** – Personal motivation, determination, and desire to accomplish something. Your fuel for change. May Your Will be indomitable when you encounter the many faces of persuasion which will tempt to sway you from your conscience.

# BIBLIOGRAPHY

1. The 11$^{th}$ Hour. Dir. Lelia Conners and Nadia Conners. Warner Independent Pictures, 2007. Film.
2. Ambrose, J. (October 13, 2019). Renewable electricity overtakes fossil fuels in UK for first time. *The Guardian.* Retrieved January 13, 2020 from https://www.google.com/amp/s/amp.theguardian.com/business/2019/oct/14/renewable-electricity-overtakes-fossil-fuels-in-UK-for-first-time
3. Arenschield, L. (December 17, 2014). Families flee out-of-control natural-gas leak at eastern Ohio fracking well. *The Columbus Dispatch.* Retrieved October 24, 2018 from https://www.dispatch.com/content/stories/local/2014/12/17/families-flee-out-of-control-natural-gas-leak.html
4. Ariza, M. (2018). As Climate Change Hits Miami, Only The Rich Will Be Able To Protect Themselves. *Huffpost.* Retrieved February 3, 2019 from https://m.huffpost.com/us/entry/us_5c13730ce4b0f60cfa27e471
5. At Least 2,000 Veterans Arrive at Standing Rock to Protest Dakota Pipeline. (December 4, 2016). *ABC News.* Retrieved March 15, 2018 from http://www.amp/abcnews.go.com/amp/US/2000-veterans-arrive-standing-rock-protest-dakota-pipeline

6. AWEA. (2013) Wind 101: The Basics of Wind Energy. Retrieved July 2016 from http://www.awea.org/Resources/Content.aspx?ItemNumber=900
7. Bambrick, G. (December 11, 2012). Fracking: Pro and Con. *Tufts Now.* Retrieved September 23, 2014 from http://now.tufts.edu/articles/fracking-pro-and-con
8. Bateman, C. (June 2010). A Colossal Fracking Mess. *Vanity Fair.* Retrieved February 10, 2015 from http://www.vanityfair.com/news/2010/06/fracking-in-pennsylvania-201006
9. *Before the Flood.* Dir. Fisher Stevens. National Geographic, 2016. Film
10. Beals, R. (August 20, 2022). *MarketWatch.* Retrieved October 13, 2022 from http://www.marketwatch.com/story/a-quarter-of-the-u-s-will-fall-inside-an-extreme-heat-belt-here-are-the-states-in-the-red-zone-11660568349?siteid=yhoof2
11. Beans,L. (January 10, 2014). Parents Outrages Over Radio Disney's Participation in Pro-Fracking Educational Tour. *EcoWatch.* Retrieved October 13, 2018 from https://www.ecowatch.com/amp/parents-outraged-over-radio-disneys-participation-in-pro-fracking-educ-1881848899
12. Benson, T. (February 25, 2019). In Los Angeles, Climate-Change Gentrification Is Already Happening. *Daily Beast.* Retrieved May 23, 2019 from https://www.thedailybeast.com/in-la-climate-change-gentrification-is-already-happening
13. Bertram, R. (November 26, 2019). Green Costa Rica is still not rosy. *Energy Transition.* Retrieved December 13, 2019 from https://energytransition.org/2019/11/green-cost-rica-is-still-not-rosy/
14. Berwyn, B. (February 12, 2018). Sea Level Rise Is Accelerating: 4 Inches Per Decade (or More) by

2100. *Inside Climate News.* Retrieved May 13, 2019 from https://insideclimatenews.org/news/11022018/sea-level-rise-accelerating-satellite-study-coastal-flood-risk-antarctica-oceans?
15. *Blood on the Mountain.* Dir. Mari-Lynn C. Evans and Jordan Freeman. Virgil Films, 2016. Film
16. *Blue Planet II.* BBC, 2017. Film
17. *The Boy Who Harnessed the Wind.* Dir. Chiwetel Ejiofor. Netflix, 2019. Film
18. Boyd, R. (March 11, 2019). Has Climate Gentrification Hit Miami? The City Plans to Find Out. *NRDC.* Retrieved May 23, 2019 from https://www.nrdc.org/stories/has-climate-gentrification-hit-miami-city-plans-find-out
19. *Brave Blue World: Racing to Solve Our Water Crisis.* Dir. Tim Neeves. Netflix, 2020. Film
20. Brown, A., Parrish, W., and Speri, A. (November 15, 2017). Dakota Access Pipeline Company Paid Mercenaries To Build Conspiracy Lawsuit Against Environmentalists. *The Intercept.* Retrieved February 13, 2018 from https://www.static.theintercept.com/amp/dakota-access-pipeline-dapl-tigerswan-energy-transfer-partners-rico-lawsuit.html
21. Brown, A. (January 9, 2018). Five Spills, Six Months In Operation: Dakota Access Track Record Highlights Unavoidable Reality – Pipelines Leak. *The Intercept.* Retrieved March 13, 2018 from https://theintercept.com/2018/01/09/dakota-access-pipeline-leak-energy-transfer-partners/
22. Bryson, B. (1998) *A Walk in the Woods: Rediscovering America on the Appalachian Trial.* Doubleday
23. Calderwood, I. (May 24, 2019). *Global Citizen.* Retrieved July 2, 2022 from http://www.globalcitizen.org/en/content/david-attenborough-plastic-health-report/

24. Carswell, C. (March 24, 2017). *Mother Jones*. Retrieved March 27, 2019 from https://www.motherjones.com/environment/2017/03/scott-pruitt-not-first-administrator-hostile-epa-mission/
25. Chow, L. (April 9, 2018). Keystone Pipeline Spilled 407K Gallons in South Dakota, Double Previous Estimate. *EcoWatch*. Retrieved April 11, 2018 from http://www.ecowatch.com/keystone-pipeline-oil-spill-2558227880.amp.html
26. Cimons, M. (December 14, 2018). Meeting Paris Agreement Targets Would Create 24 Million Jobs Globally. *Nexus Media*. Retrieved January 16, 2019 from https://nexusmedianews.com/meeting-paris-agreement-targets-would-create-24-million-jobs-globally
27. Clark, A. (November 3, 2015). How an investigative journalist helped prove a city was being poisoned with its own water. *Columbia Journalism Review*. Retrieved February 15, 2018 from https://www.cjr.org/united_states_project/flint_water_lead_curt_guyette_aclu_michigan.php
28. Concerned Health Professionals of New York. (2014, December 11). Compendium of scientific, medical, and media findings demonstrating risks and harms of fracking (unconventional gas and oil extraction) ($2^{nd}$ ed.). http://concernedhealthny.org/compendium/.
29. Cuevas, M. and Almasy, S. (November 17, 2017). Keystone Pipeline leaks 210,000 gallons of oil in South Dakota. *CNN*. Retrieved November 17, 2017 from https://www.google.com/amp/s/amp.cnn.com/cnn/2017/11/16/us/keystone-pipeline-leak/index.html
30. D'Alessandro, N. (April 7, 2014). 22 Facts About Plastic Pollution (And 10 Things We Can Do About It). *EcoWatch*. Retrieved on May 14, 2018 from https://www.ecowatch.com/22-facts-about-

plastic-pollution-and-10-things-we-can-do-about-it-1881885971.html
31. Daigle, K. and Singh, M. (August 15, 2018). As waters rise, coastal megacities like Mumbai face catastrophe. *ScienceNews*. Retrieved on May 20, 2019 from http://www.sciencenews.org/article/waters-rise-coastal-megacities-mumbai-face-catastrophe
32. Daigle, K. and Gramling, C. (January 10, 2019). Explainer: Why sea levels aren't rising at the same rate globally. *ScienceNews for Students*. Retrieved on May 20, 2019 from https://sciencenewsforstudents.org/article/explainer-why-sea-levels-rise-rate-varies-globally
33. *Dark Waters*. Dir. Todd Haynes. Focus Features, 2019. Film.
34. *The Day After Tomorrow*. Dir. Roland Emmerich. Twentieth Century Fox, 2004. Film.
35. D'Angelo, C. (April 20, 2020). *Huffpost*. 10 Years After Deepwater Horizon, The U.S. Is Even More At Risk Of A Major Oil Spill. Retrieved on April 20, 2020 from https:///m.huffpost.com/us/entry/us_5e9a369ec5b63639081e9f8b
36. D'Angelo, C. (April 22, 2019). *Huffpost*. The Climate Kids Are All Right. Retrieved on April 22, 2019 from https://m.huffpost.com/us/entry/us_5c5097ae4b082aab08abaff
37. D'Angelo, C. (March 27, 2020). *Huffpost*. States Quietly Pass Laws Criminalizing Fossil Fuel Protests Amid Coronavirus Chaos. Retrieved on March 27, 2020 from https://m.huffpost.com/us/entry/us_5e7e7570c5b6256a7a2aab41
38. D'Angelo, C. (August 12, 2019). *Huffpost*. Trump Administration Weakens Endangered Species Act Amid Global Extinction Crisis. Retrieved on

August 14, 2019 from https://m.huffpost.com/us/entry/us_5cf7b7b4e4b01713bed4df9b
39. Dembicki, G. (May 7, 2017). Dakota Access Pipeline protest movement now focuses on the money. *Mashable*. Retrieved on March 15, 2018 from https://www.amp/s/mashable.com/2017/05/07/dapl-divestment-movement-grows.amp
40. Dennis, B. (October 22, 2016). 'If I could afford to leave, I would.' In Flint, a water crisis with no end in sight. *The Washington Post*. Retrieved on February 15, 2018 from https://www.washingtonpost.com/national/health-science/if-i-could-afford-to-leave-i-would-in-flint-a-water-crisis-with-no-end-in-sight/2016/10/21/
41. Dennis, B. and Eilperin, J. (December 31, 2017). How Scott Pruitt turned the EPA into one of Trump's most powerful tools. *The Washington Times*. Retrieved December 31, 2017 from http://www.washingtonpost.com/national/health-science/under-scott-pruitt-a-year-of-tumult-and-transformation-at-epa/2017/12/26/
42. Dennis, B. and Mufson, S. (December 5, 2016). Army Corps ruling is a big win for foes of Dakota Access Pipeline. *The Washington Times*. Retrieved March 15, 2018 from https://washingtonpost.com/news/energy-environment/wp/2016/12/04/army-will-deny-easement-halting-work-on-dakota-access-pipeline/
43. Desilver, D. (January 15, 2020). Renewable energy is growing fast in the U.S., but fossil fuels still dominate. *Factank*. Retrieved February 3, 2020 from https://www.pewresearch.org/fact-tank/2020/01/15/renewable-energy-is-growing-fast-in-the-u-s-but-fossil-fuels-still-dominate
44. *The Devil We Know*. Dir. Stephanie Soechtig and Jeremy Seifert. Netflix, 2018. Film.

45. Didion, J. (October 5, 2006). Cheney: The Fatal Touch. *The New York Review*. Retrieved November 7, 2017 from http://www.nybooks.com/articles/2006/10/05/cheney-the-fatal-touch/
46. *Dirty Money*. Dir. Erin Lee Carr, Alex Gibney, Kristi Jacobson, Brian McGinn, Jesse Moss, and Fisher Stevens. Netflix, 2018. Television Series.
47. Eagle Sr., J. (November 30, 2020). An Open Letter on DAPL. *Earthjustice*. Retrieved November 30, 2020 from https://earthjustice.org/blog/2020-november/an-open-letter-on-dapl?
48. Eilperin, J. and Dennis, B. (April 27, 2019) New EPA document tells communities to brace for climate change impacts. *The Washington Post*. Retrieved May 20, 2019 from https://www.washingtonpost.com/national/health-science/new-epa-document-tells-communities-to-brace-for-climate-change-impacts/2019/04/27/
49. Eilperin, J., Mooney, C., Mufson, S., and Muyskens, J. (August 13, 2019) 2 C: Beyond The Limit Extreme climate change has arrived in America. *The Washington Post*. Retrieved August 13, 2019 from https://www.washingtonpost.com/graphics/2019/national/climate-environment/climate-change-america/
50. Ethane Cracker Plants: What Are They? (October 23, 2018) *The Climate Reality Project*. Retrieved September 30, 2019 from https://www.climaterealityproject.org/blog/ethane-cracker-plants-what-are-they
51. Fears, D. (October 21, 2018). A 14-year-long oil spill in the Gulf of Mexico verges on becoming one of the worst in U.S. history. *The Washington Post*. Retrieved October 21, 2018 from https://www.washingtonpost.com/national/health-science/a-14-year-long-oil-spill-in-the-gulf-of-mexico-verges-on-becoming-one-of-the-worst-in-us-history/2018/10/20/

52. Fears, D. (February 12, 2020). The toxic reach of Deepwater Horizon's oil spill was much larger – and deadlier – than previous estimates, a new study finds. *The Washington Post.* Retrieved February 12, 2020 from https://www.washingtonpost.com/climate-environment/2020/02/12/toxic-reach-deepwater-horizons-oil-spill-was-much-larger-deadlier-than-previous-estimates-new-study-says/
53. Florida, R. (July 5, 2018). 'Climate Gentrification' Will Deepen Urban Inequality. *Citylab.* Retrieved May 23, 2019 from https://www.citylab.com/equity/2018/07/the-reality-of-climate-gentrification/564152
54. *From Flint: Voices of a Poisoned City.* Dir. Elise Conklin. Video Project, 2016. Film.
55. *Gasland.* Dir. Josh Fox. New Video Group/HBO/International WOW Company, 2010. Film
56. *Gasland Part II.* Dir. Josh Fox. HBO, 2013. Film.
57. Gayle, D. (March 10, 2022). Millions suffering in deadly pollution 'sacrifice zones', warns UN expert. *The Guardian.* Retreived September 18, 2022 from https://amp.theguardian.com/environment/2022/mar/10/millions-suffering-in-deadly-pollution-sacrifice-zones-warns-un-expert
58. Gelfand, A. (2018). Gentrification: Climate Change's Latest Threat. *Hopkins Bloomberg Public Health Magazine.* Retrieved May 13, 2019 from https://magazine.jhsph.edu/2018/gentrification-climate-changes-latest-threat
59. *The Great Hack.* Dir. Karim Amer and Jehane Noujaim. Netflix, 2019. Film.
60. Hahn, J. (December 21, 2018). Climate Gentrification Could Exacerbate Housing Crisis in South Florida. *Sierra.* Retrieved May 23, 2019 from https://www.sierraclub.org/sierra/climate-gentrification-could-exacerbate-housing-crisis-south-florida

61. Haidar, Z. (March 23, 2015). UN Predicts Serious Water Shortages by 2030. *Weather.com*. Retrieved March 28, 2015 from http://www.weather.com/science/environment/news/water-shortage-united-nations-report
62. Hanley, S. (February 3, 2020).Costa Rica Is At Nearly 100% Renewable Energy For Electricity. *CleanTechnica*. Retrieved February 5, 2020 from https://www.google.com/amp/s/cleantechnica.com/2020/02/03/costa-rica-is-at-nearly-100-renewable-energy-for-electricity/amp/
63. *Happening: A Clean Energy Revolution.* Dir. James Redford. HBO, 2017. Film.
64. Hauter, W. (2016) *Frackopoly: The Battle for the Future of Energy and the Environment.* The New Press
65. Heinberg, R. (2013) *Snake Oil: How Fracking's False Promise of Plenty Imperils Our Future.* Post Carbon Institute
66. Helvarg, D. (October 27, 2020). I've Reported On Climate Disasters For 38 Years, Here's What We Need To Do ASAP. *Huffpost*. Retrieved October 27, 2020 from https://m.huffpost.com/us/entry/us_5fdb862cc5b6f24ae35e61ba
67. Hernandez, A. (March 6, 2018). Exodus from Puerto Rico grows as island struggles to rebound from Hurricane Maria. *The Washington Post*. Retrieved March 6, 2018 from http://www.washingtonpost.com/amphtml/national/exodus-from-puerto-rico-grows-as-island-struggles-to-rebound-from-hurricane-maria/2018/03/06
68. Hernandez, A. and McGinley, L. (May 29, 2018). Harvard study estimates thousands died in Puerto Rico because of Hurricane Maria. *The Washington Post*. Retrieved May 29, 2018 from https://www.washingtonpost.com/national/harvard-study-estimates-thousands-died-in-puerto-rico-due-to-hurricane-maria/2018/05/29

69. Hickman, L. (July 14, 2011). 'Fracking' company targets US children with colouring book. *The Guardian.* Retrieved October 13, 2018 from https://www.google.com/amp/s/amp.theguardian.com/environment/blog/2011/jul/14/gas-fracking-children-colouring-book
70. Higgins, E. (January 9, 2018). The Agency That Approves Pipelines Is About To Get A Trump-Era Overhaul. *Huffpost.* Retrieved January 9, 2018 from https://m.huffpost.com/us/entry/us
71. Hung, M. (February 10, 2018) Why This California City Is Taking On Chevron, Exxon And Shell Over Climate Change. *HuffPost.* Retrieved on February 10, 2018 from https://m.huffpost.com/us/entry/us
72. *Ice on Fire.* Dir. Leila Conners. HBO, 2019. Film
73. Ingraham, C. (September 21, 2017) Flint's lead-poisoned water had a 'horrifyingly large' effect on fetal deaths, study finds. *The Washington Post.* Retrieved February 15, 2018 from http://www.washintonpost.com/news/wonk/wp/2017/09/21/flints-lead-poisoned-water-had-a-horrifyingly-large-effect-on-fetal-deaths-study-finds/
74. *An Inconvenient Truth.* Dir. Davis Guggenheim. Participant Productions and Paramount Classics, 2006. Film
75. *An Inconvenient Sequel: Truth to Power.* Dir. Bonnie Cohen and Jon Shenk. Participant Media and Paramount Pictures, 2017. Film
76. *The Insider.* Dir. Michael Mann. Buena Vista Pictures, 1999. Film
77. Jerolmack, C. (2021) *Up to Heaven and Down to Hell: Freedom, Fracking, and Community in an American Town.* Princeton University Press
78. Kaplan, S. and Dennis, B. (February 28, 2022). Humanity has a 'brief and rapidly closing window' to avoid a hotter, deadly future, U.N. climate report says. *The Washington Post.* Retrieved April 13, 2022

from http://www.washingtonpost.com/climate-environment/2022/02/28/ipcc-united-nations-climate-change-adaptation/?utm_campaign=wp_post
79. Karklis, L., Tierney, L., and Soffen, K. (February 8, 2018) After years of drought, Cape Town is about to run out of water. *The Washington Post.* Retrieved February 8, 2018 from https://www.washingtonpost.com/graphics/2018/world/capetown-water-shortage
80. Kaufman, A. (July 6, 2018) Scott Pruitt's Replacement Is Even Worse. *Huffpost.* Retrieved July 6, 2018 from https://m.huffpost.com/us/entry/us
81. Kaufman, A. (January 16, 2019) EPA Nominee Andrew Wheeler Downplays Climate Threat At Testy Confirmation Hearing. *Huffpost.* Retrieved February 1, 2019 from https://m.huffpost.com/us/entry/us_5c3f5a1ce4b0922a21db1c11
82. Kaufman, A. (April 14, 2021). *Huffpost.* Retrieved August 17, 2021 from http://m.huffpost.com/us/entry/us_606f6a7ec5b62ff28f406914
83. Kaufman, A. (March 9, 2020). Michigan Is Facing An 'All-Out Assault On Water.' Will It Swing The State in 2020? *Huffpost.* Retrieved March 9, 2020 from https://m.huffpost.com/us/entry/us_5e610eeac5b6bd126b76fbc8/costa-rica-is-at-nearly-100-renewable-energy-for-electri
84. Kaufman, A. (February 21, 2019). Senators Not Backing Green New Deal Received On Average 7 Times As Much Fossil Fuel Cash. *Huffpost.* Retrieved February 21, 2019 from https://m.huffpost.com/us/entry/us_5c6dc9b2e4b0e2f4d8a24e83
85. Kaufman, A. and D'Angelo, C. (March 27, 2020). Trump Goes Full 'Shock Doctrine' As Pandemic Rages. *Huffpost.* Retrieved March 27, 2020 from https://m.huffpost.com/us/entry/us_5e7e3227c5b6cb9dc19f6728

86. Kaufman, A. (December 19, 2020) Ohio Quietly Passes A Bill That Could Bankrupt Churches Linked To Fossil Fuel Protests. *Huffpost.* Retrieved December 20, 2020 from https://m.huffpost.com/us/entry/us_5fdb862cc5b6f24ae35e61ba
87. Kaufman, A. (September 4, 2019). Voters Back Ban On Fracking, New Poll Finds. *Huffpost.* Retrieved September 4, 2019 from https://m.huffpost.com/us/entry/us_5d701602e4b09bbc9ef95ef9
88. Kaufman, A. (July 13, 2021). Exxon Lobbyists Paid The 6 Democrats Named In Sting Video Nearly $333,000. *Huffpost.* Retrieved October 11, 2021 from https://m.huffpost.com/us/entry/us_60ec4dceeb0910145f5075f
89. *Kiss the Ground.* Dir. Rebecca Tickell and Josh Tickell. Netflix, 2020. Film
90. Kondash, A., Lauer, N., and Vengosh, A. (August 15, 2018) The intensification of the water footprint of hydraulic fracturing. *Science Advances.* Retrieved on October 17, 2018 from https://www.scribd.com/document/386207682/Science-Advances-Intensification-of-the-Water-Footprint-of-Hydraulic-Fracturing#
91. Levin, S. (February 11, 2017). Army veterans return to Standing Rock to form a human shield against police. *The Guardian.* Retrieved March 15, 2018 from http://www.amp.theguardian.com/us-news/2017/feb/11/standing-rock-army-veterans-camp
92. Lim, X. (September 30, 2019). How Fossil Fuel Companies Are Killing Plastic Recycling. *Huffpost.* Retrieved September 30, 2019 from https://m.huffpost.com/us/entry/us_5d8e4916e4b0e9e7604c832e
93. Love, T. (December 2017). Abandoned Coal Mines Are Being Reimagined As Solar Farms. *Greenmatters.* Retrieved January 2, 2018 from http://www.greenmatters.com/renewables/2017/12/12/Z1Q5bYv/coal-solar/farms?

94. Lurie, J. (January 21, 2016). Meet the Mom Who Helped Expose Flint's Toxic Water Nightmare. *Mother Jones.* Retrieved February 15, 2018 from http://www.motherjones.com/politics/2016/01/mother-exposed-flint-lead-contamination-water-crisis
95. Lustgarten, A. (August 13, 2013). Unfair Share: How Oil and Gas Drillers Avoid Paying Royalties. *Propublica.* Retrieved October 24, 2018 from https://www.propublica.org/article/unfair-share-how-oil-and-gas-drillers-avoid-paying-royalties
96. Macfarlane, R. (2019) *Underland: A Deep Time Journey.* W. W. Norton & Company
97. McCarthy, J. (August 30, 2018). How 'Climate Gentrification' Is Changing Miami – And the Rest of the World. *Global Citizen.* Retrieved May 13, 2019 from https://www.globalcitizen.org/en/content/miami-gentrification-climate-change/
98. McGonigal, C. (September 9, 2020). Photos Show The Crazy Intensity of West Coast Wildfires. *Huffpost.* Retrieved September 11, 2020 from https://m.huffpost.com/us/entry/us_5f58ecccc5b62874bc171041
99. McKibben, B. (September 8, 2014). Bad News for Obama: Fracking May Be Worse Than Burning Coal. *Mother Jones.* Retrieved November 11, 2014 from http://m.motherjones.com/environment/2014/09/methane-fracking-obama-climate-change-bill-mckibben?
100. Miles, J. (December 22, 2014). All Naughty, No Nice: 5 Worst Fracking Industry Moments of 2014. *Food & Water Watch.* Retrieved January 17, 2015 from http://www.foodandwaterwatch.org/blogs/all-naughty-no-nice-5-worst-fracking-industry-moments-of-2014/

101. Miller, H. and D'Angelo C. (September 22, 2018). Climate Change Comes Home To Roost In North Carolina. *Huffpost*. Retrieved September 23, 2018 from http://m.huffpost.com/us/entry/us_5ba53abae4b069d5f9d2a909
102. Milman, O. (September 25, 2018). Climate gentrification: the rich can afford to move –what about the poor? *The Guardian*. Retrieved May 23, 2019 from https://www.theguardian.com/environment/2018/sep/25/climate-gentrification-phoenix-flagstaff-miami-rich-poor
103. Mooney, C. and Dennis, B. (October 3, 2018). Climate scientists are struggling to find the right words for very bad news. *The Washington Post*. Retrieved October 3, 2018 from https://www.washingtonpost.com/energy-environment/2018/10/03/climate-scientists-are-struggling-find-right-words-very-bad-news/?
104. Morrison, J. and Kordova, S. (November 18, 2019). Revolutionary recycling? A new technology turns everyday trash into plastic treasure. *The Washington Post*. Retrieved November 18, 2019 from https://www.washingtonpost.com/graphics/2019/climate-solutions/israeli-startup-ubq-turning-trash-into-plastic-products/
105. Murphy, J. (February 26, 2018). TigerSwan: Former Delta Operator sought to incite violence at the Dakota Access Pipeline. *Sofrep News*. Retrieved March 15, 2018 from https://sofrep.com/99918/tigerswan-former-delta-operator-sought-to-incite-violence-at-the-dakota-access-pipeline
106. Nicholson, L. (October 9, 2014). California aquifers contaminated with billions of gallons of fracking wastewater. *Reuters*. Retrieved December 15, 2014 from http://rt.com/usa/194620-california-aquifers-fracking-contamination/

107. Olaniran, T. (April 16, 2018). I'm a Flint resident. I'm done paying for water that is not safe. *The Washington Post.* Retrieved April 16, 2018 from http://www.washingtonpost.com/news/posteverything/wp/2018/04/16/im-a-flint-resident-im-done-paying-for-water-that-isnt-safe
108. Olorunnipa, T. and Mufson, S. (April 10, 2019). Trump signs executive orders seeking to speed up oil and gas projects. *The Washington Post.* Retrieved April 10, 2019 from https://www.washingtonpost.com/national/health-science/trump-to-issue-executive-orders-seeking-to-speed-up-oil-and-gas-projects/2019/04/09
109. Paddison, L. (March 24, 2021). Big Banks Are 'Fueling Climate Chaos' By Pouring Trillions Into Oil, Gas and Coal. *Huffpost.* Retrieved March 30, 2021 from http://m.huffpost.com/us/entry/us_605a45b8c5b6cebf58d28d52
110. Paddison, L. (December 27, 2019). 2019 Was The Year The World Burned. *Huffpost.* Retrieved December 29, 2019 from https://m.huffpost.com/us/entry/us_5dcd3f4ee4b0d43931d01baf
111. Papenfuss, M. (March 24, 2019). Oil Execs Chortle Over 'Unprecedented' Access To Trump Officials In Secret Recording. *Huffpost.* Retrieved March 30, 2019 from https://m.huffpost.com/us/entry/us_5c96efbde4b01ebeef104808
112. Parker, L. (2018). You Can Help Turn the Tide on Plastic. Here's How. *National Geographic.* Retrieved May 18, 2018 from https://www.nationalgeographic.com/magazine/2018/06/plastic-planet-solutions-waste-pollution
113. Paterson, L. (October 3, 2017). Scottish government bans fracking in landmark decision. *Independent.* Retrieved October 3, 2017 from http://www.independent.co.uk/news/uk/politics/scotland-bans-fracking-natural-gas-extrac-

tion-fossil-fuels-paul-wheelhouse-government-energy-a7980811.html
114. Phillips, A. (January 27, 2022). Biden outpaces Trump in issuing drilling permits on public lands. *The Washington Post.* Retrieved February 13, 2022 from http://www.washingtonpost.com/climate-environment/2022/01/27/oil-gas-leasing-biden-climate/?utm_campaign=wp_post
115. Pilkington, E. (December 15, 2017). A journey through a land of extreme poverty: welcome to America. *The Guardian.* Retrieved December 15, 2017 from http://www.theguardian.com/society/2017/dec/15/america-extreme-poverty-un-special-rapporteur
116. "Poisoned Water." *Nova.* Writ. Llewellyn M. Smith. Dir. Llewellyn M. Smith. PBS. 31, May 2017. Television.
117. Powers, R. (2018) *The Overstory.* W.W. Norton & Company
118. Preston, C. and Klein, R. (May 23, 2020). Are We Ready? How We Are Preparing – And Not Preparing – Kids For Climate Change. *Huffpost.* Retrieved May 23, 2020 from https://m.huffpost.com/us/entry/us_5ec6d26dc5b69106a7355661
119. Princess Mononoke. Dir. Hayao Miyazaki. Studio Ghibli, 1999. Film
120. Randall, C. (September 4, 2020). The Last-Ditch Attempt To Save America's Largest National Forest. *Huffpost.* Retrieved September 5, 2020 from https://m.huffpost.com/us/entry/us_5f4f5a3cc5b69eb5c0367e81
121. Raymond, R. (December 14, 2018). We Have 12 Years To Stop Climate Catastrophe. These Young Activists Have A Plan. *Huffpost.* Retrieved March 15, 2019 from https://m.huffpost.com/us/entry/us_5c122a7ae4b002a46c143f73
122. Richman-Abdou, K. (May 9, 2018). "Boy Genius" Is Now a Young Man With a Plan to Remove All Plastic From Oceans

by 2050. *My Modern Met.* Retrieved May 9, 2018 from https://mymodernmet.com/boyan-slat-ocean-cleanup/
123. Rosenberg, E. (December 9, 2017). 'We stood there crying': Emaciated polar bear seen in 'gut-wrenching' video and photos. *The Washington Post.* Retrieved on December 9, 2017 from http://www.washingtonpost.com/news/animalia/wp/2017/12/09/we-stood-there-crying-the-story-behind-the-emotional-video-of-a-starving-polar-bear/?utm
124. Schumaker, E. (January 23, 2018). Air Pollution Is Killing Millions Around The Globe Each Year. *Huffpost.* Retrieved January 23, 2018 from https//m.huffpost.com/us/entry/us
125. Schwartzel, E. (June 19, 2011). Color me fracked: Energy industry produces coloring book to make case for gas drilling to kids. *Pittsburg Post-Gazette.* Retrieved October 13, 2018 from https://old.post-gazette.com/pg/11170/1154547-28.stm
126. Sinclair, H. (October 17, 2017). Oil Spill in U.S. Gulf of Mexico Could Be Biggest Since Deepwater Horizon Disaster. *Newsweek.* Retrieved October 17, 2017 from http://www.newsweek.com/oil-spill-us-gulf-mexico-could-be-biggest-deepwater-horizon-disaster-687119
127. Slodysko, B. (July 13, 2018). Pence family's failed gas stations cost taxpayers $20M+. *Associated Press.* Retrieved July 13, 2018 from https://news/pence-family-gas-stations-left-145445975.html
128. Smith, D. and Welsh, B. (December 18, 2018). A million California buildings face wildfire risk. 'Extraordinary steps' are needed to protect them. *Los Angeles Times.* Retrieved May 23, 2019 from https://www.latimes.com/projects/la-me-california-buildings-in-fire-zones/

129. Smith, M. (February 23, 2017). Standing Rock Protest Camp, Once Home to Thousands, Is Razed. *The New York Times.* Retrieved on March 15, 2018 from https://mobile.nytimes.com/2017/02/23/us/standing-rock-protest-dakota-access-pipeline.html
130. Smith, M. and Bosman, J. (November 16, 2017). Keystone Pipeline Leaks 210,000 Gallons of Oil in South Dakota. *The New York Times.* Retrieved March 15, 2018 from https://www.mobile.nytimes.com/2017/11/16/us/keystone-pipeline-leaks-south-dakota.amp.html
131. The Social Dilemma. Dir. Jeff Orlowski. Netflix, 2020. Film
132. Strether, L. (August 24, 2018). Fracking, the Water Cycle, and Sacrifice Zones. *Naked Capitalism.* Retrieved October 24, 2018 from https://www.nakedcapitalism.com/2018/08/fracking-water-cycle-sacrifice-zones.html
133. Sullivan, K. (December 2, 2016). Voices from Standing Rock. *The Washington Post.* Retrieved March 15, 2018 from http://www.washingtonpost.com/sf/national/2016/12/02/voices-from-standing-rock
134. Tolentino, J. (March 19, 2019). Stepping Into The Uncanny, Unsettling World of Shen Yun. *The New Yorker.* Retrieved December 22, 2022 from http://www.newyorker.com/culture/culture-desk/stepping-into-the-uncanny-unsettling-world-of-shen-yun
135. *Triple Divide.* Dir. Joshua Pribanic and Melissa Troutman. Public Herald, 2013. Film.
136. Vagianos, A. (April 17, 2019). Teen Climate Activist Greta Thunberg To EU Lawmakers: 'I Want You To Panic'. *Huffpost.* Retrieved April 17, 2019 from https://m.huffpost.com/us/entry/us_5cb7344ce4b0ffefe3ba6287
137. Valentina, J. (March 1, 2018). Government responds to documentary film about Citarum River. *The Jakarta Post.* Retrieved May 19, 2018

from https://www.thejakartapost.com/amp/life/2018/02/28/government-responds-to-documentary-film-about-citarum-river.html
138. Vartan, S. (April 25, 2018). Remember that kid who invented a way to clean up ocean plastic? He's back, and it's happening. *Mother Nature Network*. Retrieved April 25, 2018 from https://www.mnn.com/earth-matters/wilderness-resources/blogs/amp/remember-kid-who-invented-way-clean-ocean-plastic-hes-back-and-its-happening
139. Vidal, J. (December 30, 2019). The Lost Decade: How We Awoke To Climate Change Only to Squander Every Chance To Act . *Huffpost*. Retrieved December 30, 2019 from https://m.huffpost.com/us/entry/us_5df7af92e4b0ae01a1e459d2
140. Vidal, J. (March 15, 2019). The Rapid Decline Of The Natural World Is A Crisis Even Bigger Than Climate Change. *Huffpost*. Retrieved March 15, 2019 from https://m.huffpost.com/us/entry/us_5c49e78ce4b06ba6d3bb2d44
141. *Virunga*. Dir. Orlando von Einsiedel. Netflix, 2014. Film.
142. "Voices In The Earth." *The Twilight Zone*. Writ. Alan Brennert. Dir. Curtis Harrington. CBS. 10 Jul. 1987. Television.
143. *Watermark*. Dir. Jennifer Baichwal and Edward Burtynsky. Mongrel Media, 2013. Film.
144. Watts, J. (March 19, 2018). Water shortages could affect 5bn people by 2050, UN report warns. *The Guardian*. Retrieved May 15, 2018 from https://amp.theguardian.com/environment/2018/mar/19/water-shortages-could-affect-5bn-people-by-2050-un-report-warns
145. *What Lies Upstream*. Dir. Cullen Hoback. Hyrax Films, 2017. Film
146. White, B. (September 22, 2017). These brothers wanted to fight pollution. So they paddled down the world's most polluted river in a

kayak made of plastic bottles. *The Morning Call.* Retrieved May 17, 2018 from https://www.mcall.com/opinion/white/mc-bw-lehigh-student-plastic-pollution-20170921-story.amp.html

147. Winter, C. (September 21, 2017). Nestlé Makes Billions Bottling Water It Pays Nearly Nothing For. *Bloomberg Businessweek.* Retrieved on February 17, 2018 from https://www.bloomberg.com/news/features/2017-09-21/nestl-makes-billions-bottling-water-it-pays-nearly-nothing-for

148. Witte, G., Beck, L., Dennis, B., and Kaplan, S. (March 15, 2019) School climate strikes draw thousands to the streets in cities around the globe. *The Washington Post.* Retrieved on March 15, 2019 from https://www.washingtonpost.com/world/school-climate-strikes-draw-thousands-to-the-streets-in-cities-across-the-globe/2019/03/15

149. Young, E. (November 22, 2019) Coal Knew, Too. *Huffpost.* Retrieved on November 22, 2019 from https://m.huffpost.com/us/entry/us_5dd6bbebe4b0e29d7280984f

# RESOURCES

1. The American Society For the Prevention of Cruelty to Animals: https://www.aspca.org/
2. CLEAN (the Climate Literacy and Energy Awareness Network): https://cleanet.org/index.html
3. The Climate Reality Project: https://www.climaterealityproject.org/sites/climaterealityproject.org/files/the12questionseveryclimateactivisthears_theclimaterealityproject.pdf
4. The Consensus Project: http://theconsensusproject.com
5. #DefundDAPL: http://www.defunddapl.org/defund
6. The Great Green Wall: https://www.greatgreenwall.org/about-great-green-wall/
7. The Intergovernmental Panel on Climate Change: http://ipcc.ch
8. Moms Clean Air Force: https://www.momscleanairforce.org
9. National Climate Assessment: https://nca2014.globalchange.gov
10. NASA (Global Climate Change): https://climate.nasa.gov/evidence/
11. NOAA (National Oceanic and Atmospheric Administration): https://www.noaa.gov/climate
12. Paws For Purple Hearts: https://www.pawsforpurplehearts.org/

13. Pitbulls & Addicts: http://www.pitbullsandaddicts.org
14. The Science Behind It (a project of the National Academy of Sciences): https://thesciencebehindit.org/about/
15. Water Action Decade (Sustainable Development Goals): https://www.un.org/sustainabledevelopment/water-action-decade/

Thanks for reading. I hope you found this story both educational and entertaining. If you did find it useful and/or enjoyable, could you please leave a review at the site where you bought the book?

If you bought the book directly from my author website please leave a review at: timstickle.com/reviews/ and consider signing up for my email list.

Much Love, T.L. Stickle

# ABOUT THE AUTHOR

Tim Stickle, author of Cody And The Frack-Attack Pack, received his Bachelor of Arts degree in Communications from Antioch College in Yellow Springs, OH. Born in Toledo, OH, he developed an early love of Nature from spending so much of his childhood in the area's wealth of beautiful parks and nature preserves. Incensed by the massive amount of environmental degradation in the world, Tim channels his anger into positive projects as a creative dissident. When not hiking at Oak Openings, Hocking Hills, Cuyahoga Valley, and Our National Parks, he is a red-blooded cinephile and occasional filmmaker himself.

www.ingramcontent.com/pod-product-compliance
Lightning Source LLC
Chambersburg PA
CBHW041453010526
44107CB00013B/1030